The author was born in New York City, where he attended school. He was graduated ... Teachers C ... psychology. The following year he earned his M.A. in the School of Education at New York University. Between 1954 and 1956 he studied at the University of Paris (Sorbonne) under the personal direction of the renowned Professor Jean Piaget and was there awarded a doctorate in child psychology. His doctoral thesis has been published in the French language by the Swiss publisher Delachaux and Niestle.

While obtaining his education, both here and abroad, Dr. Ostrovsky had several years in which to observe at first hand the children about whom he writes. He has taught in kindergartens, and in nursery groups. He has also served on the faculty of Vassar College, New York University and Long Island University. He is presently a full time faculty member at Queens College, New York.

Father to the Child

THE PUTNAM SERIES IN EDUCATION

A Publishing Program Dedicated to
Education as a Profession: Assessment and Planning

Consulting Editors
OLE SAND AND ELAINE COOK
Wayne State University

GETTING DOWN TO CASES: *A Problems Approach to Educational Philosophizing,* Robert L. Brackenbury, University of Southern California

THE CHILD'S WORLD: *His Social Perceptions,* Frank J. Estvan, University of Wisconsin, and Elizabeth Estvan

FIVES AT SCHOOL: *Teaching in the Kindergarten,* Elenora Moore, Wayne State University

FATHER TO THE CHILD: *Case Studies of the Experiences of a Male Teacher with Young Children,* Everett Ostrovsky, Queens College

SPURS TO CREATIVE TEACHING, Laura Zirbes, Ohio State University (Emeritus)

Father
to the Child

CASE STUDIES OF THE EXPERIENCES OF
A MALE TEACHER WITH YOUNG CHILDREN

EVERETT S. OSTROVSKY

G. P. Putnam's Sons
NEW YORK

To Erika

Foreword

I T has become almost a cliché in the field of child development that we know nothing about the effects of fathers upon their children. While there have been a few studies specifically directed toward determining the role of the father, it has been so much more convenient and feasible to study the mother-child relation that the vast majority of studies of parents are limited to the investigation of the mother.

Such a gap in our knowledge of family life should be intolerable in its own right, but, as Dr. Ostrovsky points out, there is a reason for special attention to the role of the father in modern American family life. One of the accompaniments of the technological changes of the last hundred years is the separation of industrial production from the consumption unit, the family. Consequently the major portion of the father's time is not spent in contact with other members of his own family, but rather with other bread-winners in places of employment.

Thus the father has progressively moved out of the home.

Commuting patterns may keep him away even more. The living patterns of suburbia and exurbia concentrate the interaction of father and children on the week end but provide little day-by-day opportunities for socialization, or even ordinary contact. The father's power in every-day decisions must be weakened by his greater absence, and it may even abrogate all of his traditional authority over child-rearing practices.

It is not clear, of course, just how much this generalization applies to different segments of the population and whether the trend is continuing at the present time. The farm family has certainly retained the older pattern of father participation longer than segments of society where the father works farther away from home. With shorter working hours it would be expected that the father might spend more time at home now than twenty years ago, but it also seems likely that more of the adult's recreational life takes place outside the home now than twenty years ago. Data bearing upon these questions are badly needed.

We are also unclear about the effects of reduced father participation in the family. "Mom-ism" has been condemned as a factor in the presumed deterioration of American character and has been attributed partly to the father's failure to participate more actively in family life. There is evidence that the father's presence is directly related to the effectiveness of the transmission of his values to the child. On the other hand there is also evidence that mothers do tend to transmit values that are consistent with their husband's social and occupational position even in his absence. But the problem clearly needs much more study.

For that reason a book like Dr. Ostrovsky's is particularly welcome at the present time. His efforts to trace through the consequences of father absence in a number of individual cases and to study some of the variations on this theme,—such as the widow's family, the divorcee's family, the travelling salesman's family, the phantom father—are very interesting indeed. The cases point to some of the variety of possible consequences. Some children seem to show the effects of father absence in their relations to women; some to men. Some are aggressive; some submissive. Dr. Ostrovsky has given the scientific public food for thought and interesting hypotheses for future investigations.

Alfred L. Baldwin
Cornell University
Department of Child
Development and
Family Relationships

Introduction

DOES the child of today find in the environment afforded him during his crucial early years that balance of male and female influences so necessary to his future role as an adult? Or does there exist in our present society an imbalance of these forces, with demonstrably detrimental effects on the child's emotional growth and on his adjustment to his life-role?

This book, focussing on the significance of the changed role of the father in the present-day family, raises further questions: Has the father's part in the rearing of the young child been too much minimized? What is its importance today as compared with its importance in earlier times? Has male influence upon the course of the child's development more significance than is commonly recognized in society today?

These are all questions of fundamental importance to those interested in the welfare of children. They are important to educators, child psychologists, and guidance workers because of their professional concern with the issues involved; to parents because of possible effects on family happiness; and to the enlightened public because of the broad implications such questions have for our society as a whole.

Specifically, the aim of this book is to probe the meaning of the role of the father by observing what happens to children who are to varying degrees deprived of the father's presence. Equally, the aim is to observe the effect on such children when a male adult assumes a prominent place in their environment. We shall therefore be concerned with determining how important male influence really is to the child, especially during the early years of his life; how it affects his personal and social adjustment; how it affects, too, his concept of the male role; and how this concept, once arrived at, shapes the child's behavior and attitudes in relation to his own self, to the roles of males and females among his peers and in the adult world, and to his environment in general.

The impetus to the inquiry was provided by my experiences while teaching and doing research in a number of nursery schools. Through observations of many children, day by day over the school year, and after much pondering of the reasons for the emotional difficulties of some of them, I developed a hypothesis which may be summed up as follows: that the absence of the father from the home has a crucial effect upon the developing child; that inadequate male influence involves the danger of limiting and inhibiting the child's emotional growth and producing in him more or less serious psychological disturbances; and that, therefore, male participation in early child-rearing should be increased, both within the family and outside of it, as a means of ameliorating the present imbalance between the mother and father and between the feminine and masculine influences generally.

The method of investigation was to conduct, in the light of this hypothesis, a close and detailed study of children of nursery school age. These early, most formative years in the child's life obviously constitute the most appropriate period for examining the effect on his development of so important a factor as masculine influence. They are the years when the child's attitudes and values are being formed and his conception of the world about him is being molded. The personality patterns he evolves at this time provide the base for his later adjustment. And it is at this time, therefore, that the question of the balance or lack of balance of male and female images in his environment assumes the greatest importance. At the same time there is much less of a barrier during these years between what the child thinks and feels and what he will allow himself to express. Through the spontaneity of the young child, his directness of utterance and action, the investigator can gain valuable insights into his conceptions and reactions.

In the children's spontaneous behavior, particularly, one can read the effects of previous life-experience as well as their responses to current happenings. It is in their spontaneous behavior, too, that a limiting factor such as lack of masculine influence will best reveal itself. The case-study method was therefore adopted as offering the best possibilities for fruitful investigation. The children were allowed to speak for themselves, and their reactions over extended periods of time were faithfully recorded and subsequently studied in as objective a manner as possible. The case-study of each child traces the developmental pattern of his attitudes, actions, and utterances insofar as they concern the problem under discussion. The eight cases that are here presented in this fully detailed form are highly representative.

The case-studies, in Parts II and III, make up the substance of the book. In Part I, the background of the problem is sketched, the methodology of the inquiry is explained, and the general conclusions drawn by the investigator from the whole body of data and experience are suggested. The case-studies which occupy the bulk of the book should thus be regarded as illustrating in detail conclusions already presented. Finally, the author proceeds, in Part IV, to a further analysis of the findings of the case-studies, discusses important father-child complexes, and concludes with a series of definite recommendations.

This book, then, is intended as an assessment of a family situation in our contemporary society which poses an educational problem with widely ramifying social implications. It offers suggestions toward the solution of that problem. It is hoped, particularly, that the suggestions concerned with school planning will be given careful consideration by those entrusted with the formulation of future educational policy.

Contents

Part IV—Overviews and Recommendations

PART I

BACKGROUND

Father and Child: The Setting

THOUGH the roles played by the members of the family unit have varied somewhat through the ages and in different cultural groups, the family has remained one of the primary institutions of society. Its basic structure today is what it has always been. Now, as in the past, a male and a female adult act as the protectors, providers, and educators of the immature child; and these functions of each of the adult members of the family unit are dictated by biological, psychological, and economic necessity. For the child, the family as an institution is as fundamentally important in our present-day society as it ever was in the past.

Yet if one looks back over the relatively short span of a hundred years, one notes that various changes have taken place in the structure and character of the family. And these changes, in affecting the relationships of the members of the family-unit, have had important consequences for the orientation of the child toward his parents and toward his environment. Before the period of widespread industrialization, the members of the family were more closely associated with each other and more interdependent than they are today.

Children, according to their age and capacity, often shared the work, the problems, and even the communal entertainment—musicales, group singing, parlor games, and the like—of the parents and relatives (as they still do in some present day rural communities). And relatives, or members of the extended family group, had closer ties with the child's immediate family; they were likely to be living in close proximity and to be drawn together also by a similarity of occupations and interests. For the young child, this meant an opportunity to form concrete and fairly precise conceptions of adult functions and activities. He was likely, besides, to have been a member of a large family; and in these circumstances, often with one of more of the older brothers or sisters of necessity serving as parental assistants, the child also had a greater opportunity to learn from and identify with these older brothers and sisters as well as with his parents.

The life pattern of the family, moreover, had a continuity of a sort that has become less and less characteristic of our society. This pattern was often reinforced by the fact that the children were apprenticed to the father's skills (as, of course, a few still are in the families of some craftsmen, storekeepers, and the like). They grew up helping their father in his work, as farm children still do, and were very well acquainted with the roles of both their parents. Home and work life were closely related. The working father was in close touch with his family at all times, and little conflict arose between his occupational and familial roles.

In these circumstances, the very young child soon came to appreciate his father's contribution to the welfare of the family and to sense the significance of the male role, both in the household and in the community at large. He was likely to know his father in his complete character as a man. Most important of all, he experienced a close and continuous father-and-child relationship. Thus, both father and mother were prominent as sources of influence on the child as he developed his concepts of the male and female roles in society.

In contrast, the centrifugal tendencies of family life in today's urban society are all too obvious. The activities of various members of the family are likely to be pursued for the most part outside the home and are seldom such as to allow all members to participate in them. The ties of the extended family group have likewise weakened. The members are often widely scattered. Wide geographical distribution for reasons of employment is common; and occupations and interests tend to vary greatly. Smaller living quarters, too, have contributed to making the modern family a less extended unit.

Thus, the child in modern life does not have the same sense of sharing in the round of adult life and activities as did his earlier counterpart; nor does he have the extended family group to rely upon for affection and supplementary models for imitation. He does not have the same opportunity to participate in the work of his parents or to appreciate fully the significance of their respective functions.

The father's work, especially, is hardly ever shared in by his children. As a result of the demands of industrialized society, men work mostly away from home, the father for the greater part of the day operates in a different sphere from that of the rest of the family, and his occupational functions are consequently "dehumanized" for the other members of the family.

The young child, particularly, has little concrete grasp of his father's work role. With no tangible model before him, he can only picture his father's work-life in an abstract way. Since he comprehends mostly by sight and by tactile activity he cannot be expected to form a clear and meaningful picture through mere verbal description of what his father does during the greater part of the day. He has no frame of reference in his own experience within which he can place his father's working life.

Nor does the young child have in most cases a sufficiently close and continuous emotional relationship with his father. Most fathers in urban and suburban families are at home only a few waking hours during the weekday; and the distribution of these hours and the father's frequent weariness after work and travel do not contribute to making them the most propitious time for cultivating a sound parent-child relationship. This is especially so when the child is young and his schedule does not coincide very well with the period of the father's presence in the home. In general, the physical basis for a strong attachment is too restricted. Since the father's presence in the home and his participation in family life are limited, the child's view of him tends to be limited also.

The father's infrequent presence within the family circle has forced him, especially in his relationship with the pre-school child, to delegate most of his parental functions to the mother. She often takes over disciplining, which in the past was one of the traditional functions of the father. She is likely, in addition, to be supplying almost all the companionship, affection, and guidance which the modern child receives within the family group. (An incidental result of all this is that the family structure itself tends to be further weakened by the fact that the parents do not jointly share in the responsibilities of child-rearing.) The mother retains her role in bringing up the youngster far beyond the years when biological necessity might make it mandatory that she do so. The problem is aggravated by the fact that because of the infrequent presence of the father, the child finds he is not able to rely on him as he can on his mother for the fulfillment of his everyday needs. Not surprisingly, the mother usually comes to be preferred by the child as a source of reassurance, affection, and help. The father, having already lost much of his status in the child's mind as the representative male figure and as the symbol of authority, falls still further into the background.

However dominant the role of the male adult in our society may be in other respects, his participation in child-rearing is on the whole a minor one. The home from which the male parent is missing completely, through death, divorce, or permanent separation merely represents an extreme case of the father-absenteeism that is a far too prevalent characteristic of our society.

Since families now are smaller and less closely associated with the community or the extended family group, a specialization has been forced upon the parental figures. Although parents in the modern family have an even greater responsibility in fulfilling their function, since they are now the principal and often the only male or female images which the child can emulate in his early years, we find that society now sets a less well-defined pattern for them to follow than it did in the past. In the typical patriarchal family of a century ago, distinctive roles of the father and the mother were dictated by tradition, but they have grown less clear with time.

The father does not supply the child with a sex-model of the male to as great an extent as the mother does of the female. For the boy, this is important because, for reasons of identification, he should have an understanding of his father's role and a well-rounded conception of the male figure on which to pattern his own behavior. And it is also important for the girl to have a good understanding of the father and to establish a close relationship with him in order that she may properly develop in a mixed male and female society.

Another factor in present-day paucity of adequate father-child relationship is the remote and sometimes almost embarrassed attitude of fathers, and men generally, toward young children. This attitude is caused in part by the lack of sufficient experience in being around children. But it is due also to an unfortunate tendency in our society to repress affectionate playfulness and tender feelings on the part of men. This attitude, which discourages any attempt at expression of the full range of an adult male's feelings, is likely enough to be perpetuated in the child, who will emulate a negative attitude as quickly as a positive.

The danger to the father himself is that he may by his behavior further estrange himself from his family and that he may finally come to feel like an outsider when he is with those to whom he wishes to be closest. The father thus misses a great deal of the adventure and joy of watching a child develop under one's care and guidance.

Nor, unfortunately, has the strict authority which yesterday's father exercised been replaced by the constructive guidance and companionship the modern father is more conditioned to offer. It is true that the father tends to take a greater interest in the upbringing of his children when they have grown up a bit and the relationship can take place on a more adult and companionable plane; but in his common neglect of those important years of early childhood, a great loss is incurred by parent and child. By the time the father is ready to establish a close relationship with the child, the child too often has been conditioned to the same lack of ease and rapport which the father has shown in the past.

So we return to the paradoxical situation that although the child in today's industrial society is more than ever dependent upon his parents alone for identification figures, the representative of the male parental role is too ofen unable, because of the conditions and mores of society, to meet even a major part of the demands made upon him. The original importance of the father's contribution to family life has not lessened, but the father's ability to fulfill his parental functions properly has been steadily decreasing,

Even before the age of two, the child is prepared to include the father within his realm of experience, for already his dependence upon the mother is beginning to weaken. What is more, in terms of the child's perception of the world, he is now able to encompass more than the original mother-unit. From this time on, the father can become increasingly important in the child's emotional life and the structure of his personality. He can as time goes by aid the child in understanding his own sex-role, in helping him to establish his identity as one of the components of the family structure, in forming his attitudes towards authority, in helping him to anticipate and respond to the expectations of both his parents, and in giving him emotional security and a feeling of his own worth. The father can also help the child set up goals and ideals which will aid him in his adjustment to the outside world. The father not only can do all this, he should and must if his child is to have the advantages that are his due.

The child's behavior in the very early years usually gives strong indications of his deeply-felt need for male influence in his life. He is likely to grasp at every opportunity to establish more extensive contacts with male adults. His especial attraction to male figures of authority and to the more obvious representatives of the masculine work role is easily observable. Hence the well-known appeal to the young child of policemen, firemen, garbage collectors, and other men who are engaged in occupations which represent the sort of masculine work role with which he is familar in his everyday life.

Young children, including female children, are likely to imitate these men in their games and play-acting; they sense adventure and excitement in such occupations which is totally absent in notions of their own fathers' work in the world. In this and many other ways, the child evinces a desire to establish fuller and more concrete relationships with male adults than can be provided by a father who is too often absent.

Because of minimal presence of the father, present-day family life does not supply the child to a sufficient extent with a male sex-image as clearly defined and as meaningful as the female image provided by the mother and other women with whom the child constantly comes in contact; it does not supply him with the experience and knowledge he needs to form adequate conceptions of his own sex-role. Ideally, a child should be able to form for himself a secure and knowledgeable view of the world and to achieve little by little a clear conception of his own role in it. For optimum development, his psychological environment must be a well-balanced one: it must be a world in which both the male and female principles are adequately represented and where masculine and feminine qualities are composites of life experience. In a family which cannot provide this sort of environment, the child is often in difficult straits, not only in respect to his own growth and development, but also in terms of his adjustment to his peers and to the outside world in general.

Under present conditions his situation does not improve when he steps from the home into the school environment. Male-female imbalance will, in fact, be further increased, for the nursery schools now employ women as teachers almost exclusively and this pattern of female predominance, moreover, is continued in only slightly less degree during the years of elementary schooling.

The following chapters will illustrate through case-study materials the effects of reduced influence of the father and other adult males on the present-day child. It is natural to assume that since parents play such a significant part in the child's emotional growth, in the evolution of his sense of values, and in his conception of himself and of his future role in life, the relatively infrequent presence or complete absence of one of them will militate strongly against the child's optimum development. If we premise the desirability of both parents being equally involved and equally influential in the furthering of the child's personality development, the dangers inherent in the infrequent presence and insufficient influence of the father will be obvious enough.

The case studies that follow show how children reveal in

their behavior the limitations put upon their development by a lack of sufficient male influence in their lives. They further show that these detrimental effects vary according to the quality and quantity of the child's contact with the father, and their presentation has therefore been so arranged as to illustrate this gradation. We thus consider first the cases of children whose fathers are present in the home to an inadequate degree and then move on to consider cases in which children are almost entirely or are entirely deprived of their fathers' presence. In these latter cases, as we shall see, the consequences can be so profound as to produce a psychological crisis in the young child.

Topics for Discussion

Chapter 1 *Father and Child: The Setting*
1. In what ways may the different environmental settings of urban and suburban living influence the child?
2. What differences might one expect to find between the father's role in urban and in suburban life? What factors might determine these differences?
3. Do you think parental expectations usually differ for male and female children? Have these expectations changed in the last 50 years?
4. Do you think that the school and the community act as a kind of "extended family"?
5. Do you expect father absenteeism to increase or decrease in the future? Upon what factors would you base your answer?

The Child Under Study: Methods and Procedures

THE case history approach was chosen for this book because such an approach is likely to provide the most revealing insight into the child's entire personality structure. The child can be observed as an entity, over an extended period of time, and within a variety of situations; and the observer can gain fuller knowledge and deeper perspective than if he used an approach which attempted to focus on specific or isolated segments of the child's personality.

This approach offers, in fact, the best means of achieving the two-fold purpose of this book: to examine the specific psychological effects upon the child of too little contact with the father and other male adults, and to observe the reactions of such a child when he is subjected to consistent male influence. It permits detailed observation of changes in behavior and facilitates recognition of manifest stages in the evolution of emotional problems. It provides for correlating of observations and permits their evaluation in terms of the child's more or less complete behavior pattern.

It is advantageous, besides, in that the child is observed in a series of "natural" situations and not in a specifically created, predetermined set of circumstances. His feelings and ideas are expressed in the course of incidents which are a part of his day-to-day experience and in surroundings that are familiar and thus conducive to spontaneous action.

Most of the case study material presented here was obtained during the course of various forms of projective play. A child's actions and utterances while engaged in such play are a most revealing indicator of the basic needs and desires which underlie his behavior.

All forms of projective play have been found exceedingly useful in this respect, but dramatic-play episodes are particularly so. They encompass a broad range of behavior and are thus most likely to expose fully the child's behavioral pattern. By his movements, gestures, facial expressions, verbal responses, and use of manipulative material during dramatic-play the child reveals the whole configuration of his personality. In dramatic-play, what is more, he is not merely expressing his personal conceptions in an inanimate environment; he has the opportunity, also, to react to the other children who participate with him and who can stimulate, support, or challenge him.

The dramatic-play area is a real-life stage. Each child becomes part of a dynamic group and can thus observe the effects of his behavior on others. He can experience the feelings his behavior arouses in himself and the responses it calls forth from others. To portray his part with meaning, moreover, he must reveal his understanding of the roles of others. He is motivated by his own personality as well, as he utilizes his experiences and attitudes in projecting them into an actual situation.

Dramatic-play becomes for the child a scaled-down version of real life. It enables him to cope with and even command situations which, on a larger scale, would tend to overpower him. He can feel free, for instance, to react to an adult as represented by another child in the way he would like to react toward an actual adult, without having to face the repercussions of real life adult-child relations. Dramatic-play is, therefore, a valuable vehicle for projection, compensation, and liberation of a child, as well as being an excellent technique for purposes of observation.

Those not familiar with the technique of dramatic-play as practiced in many nursery schools may be interested in a brief description of the physical arrangements and materials used. The area of activity is generally a corner or section of the playroom set apart by a screen, low cupboard, or the like, from other room activities. It should provide the children with enough sense of seclusion to encourage freedom of expression and yet be accessible enough to allow them to enter and leave at will and to encourage others to join the activity. The teacher or observer must be able to take up a position from which he can observe the children unobtrusively and still be able to take careful note of their actions.

The dramatic-play area is equipped with child-sized furniture (tables, chairs, a cot or two, a doll carriage, a kitchen stove, a basin or sink, movable screens, perhaps also a clock, a picture on the wall, a vase), kitchen and cleaning equipment (dishes, silverware, a washline, clothespins, soap powder, brooms, mops, pails), toilet articles (mirror, combs, brushes, a razor without blade, shaving brush and soap, perhaps a lipstick and hairpins), various articles of men's and women's clothing, a briefcase, newspapers, remnants of material to be draped for any desired effect, various types of dolls (complete with clothing, bottles, nipples, bedding, etc.), a toy animal or two, and the first-aid supplies (band-aids, bandages, mercurochrome), which children love to use. The materials provided should not, however, be so plentiful that little opportunity is left for the child to imagine and innovate.

In addition to dramatic play, other projective activities were utilized for observation purposes: stories told by the children, doll play, group discussions, etc. Conversations overheard during the course of the school day were also revelatory. Finally, interviews with parents and occasional visits to the home provided additional information which was recorded and studied.

The first four of the cases presented in the following chapters deal with children who come from homes which can be considered normal, homes, that is, where the two parents are present and where no serious emotional conflict exists within the family circle. Here we shall be dealing with the effects upon the child of the customary absence of the father from the home as he does his work in our present-day society.

The detrimental effects which may be produced by a paucity of male influence will reveal themselves in a more aggravated form in children who come from homes where the father is away even more often than is usual in our society or is absent entirely, or where his occasional presence is surrounded by a great deal of emotional tension. The last four cases presented below deal with children who come from such broken homes. The term "broken homes" includes homes disrupted by divorce, separation, desertion, death or long illness of one of the parents, extended absence of the father for reasons of employment or during periods of war, or through imprisonment or institutionalization. Nor should we omit from this category the home in which, though both parents are physically present, the emotional gulf between them is so great as to have destroyed all sense of family unity; in such instances, the effects may be as serious as in the case of outright family breakdown.

Since the young child usually remains with the mother when family disruption takes place, it is the paternal influence that is eliminated or excessively reduced. Even when the child remains with the father, he seldom has sufficiently frequent contact with him; he is usually left to the care of women, and all the more so, if the father is divorced and in the process of forming a new life for himself. Contacts with male friends of the family, relatives, and neighbors may, of course, be of value since they in some measure provide the masculine influence which is generally lacking in a broken home. But in most cases, the infrequency and inconsistency of these contacts render them insufficient for filling this need.

Central to the theme of this book is the hypothesis that the nursery school can provide a means of dealing constructively with the problem of absence of the masculine figure in the life of the very young child by including men as well as women on its staff. It is further suggested that there should also be increased employment of men teachers in elementary schools. Since the time spent by a child in school covers a large portion of his day, the importance of his being exposed during school hours to male as well as female influence should not be underestimated.

Topics for Discussion

Chapter 2 *The Child Under Study:*
         Methods and Procedures

1. In what ways might play reflect a child's growth and development?
2. What might various roles taken by children in dramatic play indicate about their (a) personality (b) home life?
3. How may the fantasy that sometimes enters the child's play aid him in working out his problems?
4. How might the emotional state of a child effect (a) his play (b) his language (c) his motor-activity?
5. How might an original story told by a child give insight into his preoccupations and problems and his view of himself and the world?

PART II

CHILDREN WITH PART TIME FATHERS

Case 1

Lucy:

The Salesman's Daughter

BACKGROUND: *Lucy: 4.8 years at entrance; above average intelligence; an only child; mother 32, father 36; both parents work; maternal grandmother occasionally takes care of child; 1 year previous nursery school experience; normal birth, breast-fed; good physical health.*

Upon entering the group, Lucy examined various playthings, spoke to one or two children, and then told her mother, "I know this place now; you don't have to stay with me." To me, her first remark was, "Are you really going to be the teacher?" A few moments later, she said to another child, "Did you see that big tall man? He's the teacher." The other child answered, "He's got the longest legs I ever saw." They both laughed, and Lucy looked up to see what my reaction would be.

Her surprise at finding a man as her teacher soon gave way to a strong attachment. She insisted that I remain near her during the rest period, saying, for instance, "I need you here. You make a big shadow and keep the light out of my eyes." (The lights were out and the shades half drawn as usual during rest period.) And she would employ similar ruses to sit next to me at the lunch table, claiming, for example, "This yellow chair is mine. I was here long ago." If the chair beside me was already occupied, she would divert the attention of the child sitting in it by saying something like, "Isn't that your mother out in the hallway?" When the child got up, she would quickly claim the seat.

She often called me for help in some activity, especially if I were occupied with other children. To be sure of gaining my attention, she would sometimes resort to whining or baby-talk and sometimes challenge me imperiously. Thus, during one of the first dramatic play episodes, in which Lucy was the "mother," and the youngest girl in the group the "baby," she bottle-fed the "baby" and arranged the covers. Suddenly she stopped, looked up, and called: "Hey man, come to see my baby. I think it's feeling sick." Then she added defiantly, "Or are you too busy mixing those silly paints?" When I came over to look at the "baby," she became very much excited, giggled, pulled the covers off the child, dropped the bottle on the floor, and finally ran and hid behind the cupboard.

In general, Lucy showed that she wanted a great deal of my attention. Yet she was not able to ask for it in a direct manner and used various diversionary devices instead. When the attention was given her, she sometimes showed an over-reaction to it: she became confused and not quite capable of handling the situation, often resorting to another device, such as the hide-and-seek routine, to cover her emotion.

Her attitude toward my assistant, a woman, was calmer.

She did not employ baby-talk or ruses to gain her attention. She did not often ask her for help and, although she showed definite signs of liking her, seemed to accept her presence in a more matter-of-fact way.

Lucy's reaction to the boys in the group was generally two-fold. Wishing to have them participate in games, she would either assume a coy, somewhat helpless look, or else she would challenge them and become angry if they did not respond. An illustration of this behavior can be seen in the following dramatic play episode:

Lucy was dressed to go shopping, wearing coat, hat, and high heel shoes and carrying a marketing bag. The same little girl as before accompanied her as her "baby." They built an imaginary store out of a wooden box, with a bell for a cash register, pebbles for money, and so on. Then they entered through the imaginary street door, knocked on the counter, and called, "Hey, grocery man, where are you? We want some potatoes and some chocolate pudding." When there was no answer, Lucy impatiently rang the bell and remarked: "He ought to hear that, unless he's sleeping on both ears." The girls looked at each other and laughed. Then Lucy said, "You stay right here. I'm going to see if I can wake him up, even if he snores." She imitated the sound of loud snoring, left the store and went over to a boy playing nearby, saying: "Could you help my baby and me? We haven't eaten for fourteen days and the grocery man is asleep." The boy, however, was so busy building a bridge out of blocks that he did not answer or bother to look up. Lucy made a face, shrugged her shoulders, and walked away. Soon another boy caught her eye. This time she approached him determinedly and tapped him on the shoulder: "You're coming with me. I need a grocery man." He started to get up from the floor, somewhat puzzled; but then another boy called him to look at a boat he had made and he turned on his heel, leaving Lucy standing there, with no grocery man. She became very angry, stamped her foot, and went over to the first boy and kicked his elaborate block construction across the floor. She then grabbed the "baby's" hand, saying, "I don't like this rotten game. Let's do something else," and went stomping "home."

Lucy was much more even-tempered towards the girls. If she wished them to play with her, she asked them directly, without resorting to subterfuge; and if they did not wish to join her game, she would either join theirs or find some other activity without much ado.

I was absent for a few days about a month after Lucy entered school. When I returned, my assistant told me that Lucy had seemed somewhat upset, had asked frequently about me, had not rested very well, and had fought with boys on two occasions without provocation.

When Lucy saw me again she said, "Where were you all this time? I thought you were gone for good." That day she insisted on staying close to me all day, remarking several times, "I have to stay here and watch you so you don't go away again." She also asked me privately whether I didn't like her better than all the other children in the group.

Later she brought me some paintings she had done during my absence. One in particular seemed to preoccupy her. She volunteered the explanation that it depicted "a girl under an umbrella, and it's raining. And that's a man. The wind is blowing him into a cloud. Now you can't see him, only his eyes. That's his coat lying in the puddle next to the girl, and there's a dog and he's going to eat up the coat."

Lucy's remarks to me, together with her explanation of

the painting, reflected worry at my absence, an attempt to prevent any such future absence by pretending that she must supervise me (implying, perhaps, that I could not be trusted to stay), and also (as reflected in the desire to punish the man's coat which was going to be eaten by the dog) an indirect hostility.

A conference with Lucy's mother indicated certain similarities between the child's attitude toward me and her response to her father. She expressed worry over his absences, which occurred several days at a time at various intervals, since he worked as a traveling salesman. The child had a habit of hiding the father's hat in the morning, saying to her mother, "Now he can't go away," or "If it rains, he'll be sorry he left." She showed dismay if her father succeeded in finding the hat. She also alternated this behavior with a show of helplessness, declaring that she could not dress herself without her father's help, whereas actually she had long been able to do so except for the tying of her shoelaces. From the mother's attitude I could gather that both parents were understanding and sympathetic.

Lucy's wishes in regard to her father, and perhaps to me as a father substitute, were revealed one afternoon in a story she told to a few of the children. The story was about a man who had gone out fishing with a big net. He didn't catch any fish; instead the first thing he caught was a hamster (we had hamsters as pets in the schoolroom), then an elephant, a pig, a pair of big boots, a rabbit, and, finally, a monkey. When he thought he was all finished catching things, he suddenly felt the net move and something wriggle in it. He looked into the net and found a little girl named Frances. The man was so surprised that he started to laugh, and he laughed until his belly ached. All the animals, and even the big boots, wanted to go home with the man, but he said he couldn't take them because they wouldn't all fit in the basket. So they all cried, but the one who cried the loudest was the little girl. So he took her home in his basket.

Lucy's story expressed her wish to be wanted by the "fisherman" in preference to all the other "animals." She achieved this wish in the story by a greater display of distress than the others. Her helplessness is established by the fact that she does not even walk home with the man, but is carried, the way a much younger child would be. In actual life, Lucy was not able to express her wish for attention or affection directly, as is shown by her finding it necessary to hide her father's hat and to use various devices to keep me near her. In the story, the little girl, Frances, was able to convey to the "fisherman" her wish that he should choose her to take home. Nevertheless, even in this case, her wish is not actually verbalized. She reverts to an infantile form of expression, crying, to achieve the desired results, much in the same way as she pretended that she could not dress herself when she was able by this device to gain the attention or retain the presence of her father.

Toward the end of the school year some changes were noted in Lucy's behavior. She seemed less anxious to draw my attention, and she was able to join the boys in games with greater self-confidence and without having to resort so often to devices for gaining attention. As she became less demanding toward me, she transferred some of her desire for adult concern to the woman teacher. This lessening of tension was also observed at home, and an interview with the child's mother revealed that her father had recently been away less often on business trips and so had been able to spend more time with her than before.

One morning at about this time, Lucy was sitting among several dolls in the dramatic corner. She had a shawl about her shoulders and was feeding two of the dolls, which were placed side by side on a chair. She hummed to them, changed their clothes, and then started to sing them a nursery rhyme:

> Bye baby bunting
> Daddy's gone a-hunting.

She repeated the last phrase several times, then stopped and seemed to be considering the words. She took one of the dolls on her lap, stroked its head, and said, "Your daddy's gone out hunting to Mexico and maybe even to New Jersey. He went out hunting to bring us good things for dinner to-night." She then picked up the second doll and said, "Now, I don't want you to cry. You're a big girl now." She thought for a while, then added: "Nothing is going to happen to him. He didn't really go to New Jersey. He only went downtown to the office. And there are no lions and tigers there. There, you drink your milk."

Lucy was, of course, here displaying some of her anxieties at her father's absences, as she had earlier shown concern over my absence.

In her story of the fisherman, the man takes the child home with him, whereas the hunter leaves the child behind. In the "grocery store" episode, the grocer is not even present to fulfill the most basic needs. During the first part of her speech to the doll, Lucy expresses some of the primitive notions of danger, placing the father in an unknown place, a jungle filled with lions and tigers, in sections of the country which to her seem extremely remote. When the doll begins to cry, using the same manner of expressing her distress as

little Frances in the story of the fisherman, Lucy reasons
with her and implies that she is a big girl now, accessible
to rational understanding.

This rational understanding she herself voices by changing the fear-inspiring jungle to a safe and innocuous "office
downtown" and adding the explanation that the father has
gone away only to bring back food for his family and will
return. He has now become the family provider in contrast
to the faithless grocery man who did not appear at a time
of need. This acknowledgment of being able to predict the
return of the father denotes a change in Lucy's attitude; it
may account in some measure for her ability to feel confident
enough of my presence not to have to resort any longer to
devious means of getting attention. The father's increased
presence at home had apparently been reassuring to Lucy
and had given her a more realistic view of him as well as a
greater sense of security.

Summary:

Lucy presents the picture of an affectionate, imaginative
child who wishes to relate to and include in her daily experiences men and women and boys and girls. Because of
her more frequent contact with women, she showed greater
ease and facility in her behavior toward them: she did not
cling to her mother or the woman teacher, nor did she have
to assure herself of their interest in her. Development of a
similar healthy attitude toward her father and myself and
toward the boys in the group, had, however, been thwarted
by her father's frequent absence. Lucy consequently felt the
need to reassure herself in this domain, to test reactions,
and to resort to devices such as pretended helplessness,
ruses, and attempts to assure the father's presence and mine

by trying to assume a dominating attitude. When she was disappointed, as when her father had to be away for a few days or when I had to be absent from school, she showed dismay mingled with disguised hostility.

Lucy's dramatic play and her use of the other realms of projective expression reveal her particular needs. The very fact that she was able to externalize her own needs and desires by projecting them into an imaginative form shows that these needs and desires had not been entirely repressed. She was not yet able to express them directly, in actual life; hence her belief that various devices were necessary to convey these needs, which was coupled with a lack of confidence that these devices would always be able to secure the desired results. And this lack of confidence itself tended to increase her anxiety.

The changes in Lucy's behavior by the end of the school year indicate the probable development of a more secure attitude in regard to men. One of the factors which contributed to this change in her personality was her ability to transfer her feelings and uncertainties concerning her father to me; she was thus enabled to resolve these problems in the atmosphere of a consistent and predictable relationship. That her father eventually was able to spend more time with her and that he proved no less understanding and sympathetic to Lucy's needs were also important factors in her development. My role was not that of a substitute father, but rather that of another man to whom the child could relate. She could enact her difficulties before me as well as find in me a modifying agent for her preconceived ideas about the role and function of men.

In addition, of course, all the forces which were part of Lucy's experiences during the year—the home, the school, the other children, and the general freedom of expression allowed her and the encouragement given her—contributed to the beginning of a more complete integration and a better capacity to cope with those factors which had previously limited her development.

TOPICS FOR DISCUSSION

Chapter 3 *Lucy*

1. How should indirect expressions of hostility be handled by a teacher? By the parent?
2. What might the use of ruses on the part of a child indicate to us? Should they be treated as deliberate deceit or as an indication of the child's preoccupations? What role does motivation play in regard to the use of ruses?
3. Are attention getting devices such as those used by Lucy unusual or are they rather common among children?

Case 2
Paul:
The Spartan Boy

BACKGROUND: *Paul: 5.0 years at entrance; mother 38, father 42; both working; one older sister, age 12; average intelligence; good coordination; tall for his age; normal birth, bottle-fed; no previous nursery school background; good physical health.*

Paul seemed somewhat withdrawn in his new environment. He spoke little. Although he went along with the activities of the group, he seemed to prefer to work individually. He did not show much response to the women teacher or to the girls in the group. If there was an attempt on the part of the former to help him or if he were asked if he needed help, he would refuse very directly, saying; "I can do it myself." Although he displayed much the same attitude toward me, if I asked him to help me, he always complied.

It was not until about two weeks had elapsed that Paul's behavior began to change. This happened at a time when most of the youngsters had begun to form individual or group relationships and to show definite preferences for certain children. Now Paul began to show indications of restlessness. He began asserting himself and taking the dominant part in games and activities whenever he could.

His relation to me also underwent a change. He challenged my guidance more and more, at times trying himself to assume the role of teacher. One day, for example, as we were working in the wood shop and I was showing one of the boys how to use a saw, Paul came over, grabbed the saw from my hand, and said, "I know how to do that. I'll show him the way." When he tried to do so, the saw blade got wedged in the wood. He then tried to persuade the other child to abandon the activity, telling him, "This is no fun. Come with me and I'll show you something much better." When the child declined to go, he pushed him and left.

Another time, while I was telling a story to the entire group, I noticed that Paul had begun to whisper to the children near him. He had soon formed a small group of four children to whom he was beginning to tell a story. When I stopped and asked him whether he wanted to help me tell stories by taking his group of children to another side of the room and continuing his story there, he answered, "No, I want to tell your story. I know exactly how it goes." He looked around at the other children as if wondering what their reaction would be. When I told him that I would allow him to tell the story, he added, "Well, then I have to sit where you are sitting." I gave him the chair and sat down on the side.

He began the story, telling of a ferocious warrior with a tremendous spear, who, when anyone bothered him, "killed him dead." All the animals were his friends, because they knew that he could help them if they got into trouble. One day, the warrior was going for a walk and he met a giant, who said to him, "Get out of my way, or I'll kick you." So the warrior took his gun and threw it away. Then he said to the giant, "I don't even need my gun to kill you." And he picked up the giant and threw him way up into the trees, so high that even the birds couldn't see him. And he wasn't even tired. All of a sudden, he heard somebody crying. When the big warrior looked, he saw a fox sitting on the grass. He was crying because he had been afraid for the warrior. He cried so hard, and his tears were so big, that even his feet got all wet. At this point Paul laughed, and so did the children. Then Paul decided he did not want to continue the story.

I began to notice at this time a certain characteristic of Paul's behavior: he would show no emotion himself and he seemed confused when emotion was displayed by others. One day, he tripped and fell on some blocks and hit his head. Although he held his head, gritted his teeth, and scowled, he did not cry as most children of his age would have down. When I tried to help him off the floor and say a few comforting words to him, he shook off my arm immediately and said, holding back his tears, "I can get up myself. Get away!"

Another time, while the children were playing with one of our hamsters, a male, a small block of wood accidentally fell on the animal's foot. He shrieked for a moment and then hid under some papers. Paul was standing near by. He seemed perplexed and said to me, "He's a man-hamster, and men shouldn't cry." When I said, "Even men sometimes cry when they feel very bad," he seemed surprised and retorted, "No, you're wrong. Not a real man wouldn't."

It can be seen from Paul's behavior that his main concern was to prove to himself and to those about him that he was independent, powerful, and capable of performing adult acts, that he was indeed capable of superhuman feats, even as the "ferocious warrior" in the story was able to throw a giant up into the trees "without even feeling tired." His behavior also revealed he did not wish to show emotion even when emotion was warranted, because to do so would be unmanly.

One day I had brought some shaving equipment to school. The children were very much interested in it, and there was furious activity in the dramatic corner in front of our one mirror. The boys took turns "shaving," and some of the girls did too. (On the whole, the girls preferred shaving their legs.) Paul went through elaborate preparations, lathered his whole face, including his nose and some of his hair, and then very carefully began to "shave." He made it seem as though it were very difficult to cut through his bristles, declaring, "This is a hard job. My beard is tougher than any of yours. It's so tough that nobody can touch my face without sticking himself." At this, one of the girls said, "Aw, you're always so tough. That's why I don't like to play with you." "Who wants to play with girls anyway?" was Paul's retort. "Girls are silly."

Paul had become attached to one of the hamsters. He fed him, cleaned his cage, and made certain that none of the children handled him roughly, warning them, "You'd better be careful. He's small. Look how small his feet are." When the children had left and he was sure that they could not observe him, he stroked the animal and said to him, "I'll take care of you. If anybody hurts you, I'll beat 'em up."

The instances illustrate again Paul's emphasis on physical prowess, his insistence on his invulnerability (his imaginary beard, tougher than anyone else's, protects him like armor), and his scorn of girls as inferior or at least "silly." On the other hand, we see revealed a side of Paul's character which is much softer and warmer than he would like to admit. His concern for the hamster and his wish to protect him from harm is, however, coupled with a threat to the other children in the best "manly" tradition.

Similar reaction was noted about this time in Paul's concern for smaller children, whom he helped and encouraged on the swings and the climbing apparatus. His solicitude for them was usually coupled with admonitions to the other children. To one of the older boys, for instance, he said, "You'd better not take the swing away from Frank or you'll have to answer to Big Chief War-horse." (Paul was an Indian chief that day, wearing a paper headdress he had made.) This sort of behavior occurred when there were many children about. When Paul was alone with one child, his attitude was much more gentle, and he could show concern, without a need to challenge anyone.

In my conferences with Paul's parents I found them disinclined to talk freely about him. On one occasion, however, the mother admitted that he was difficult at home. She also mentioned, in reference to a current cold which was keeping Paul at home, that he was used to being in the house alone, since his father wished him to become as independent as possible. Ever since he had been four years old he had been expected to take care of his own needs. Other meetings with the father confirmed that his participation in the child's life was mainly directed toward making him as self-reliant as possible, emphasizing male characteristics of stoicism and attempting to "harden his character."

I noticed, however, that after a time Paul's disdain, or at

least his pretended disdain, for a show of feeling began to lessen somewhat. This was clearly illustrated when one child accidentally hit his finger with a hammer and cried, "Ow!" Another child came over and asked what had happened. Paul, who had been observing the incident, volunteered the explanation, "He hurt his finger. Let's put some cold water on it." He made no attempt to show disdain at the child's expression of pain.

At another time he went even further. One of the girls had become very frightened by a story a friend of hers had invented. She began to sob and I went over to comfort her and stroke her head. Paul saw me do this and came over. When the little girl had stopped crying, he asked, "Why were you stroking her head?" "Because she was afraid," I replied, "and it made her feel better." He said nothing and went back to his play. But when I turned around a few moments later, I saw that Paul had left his toys and was stroking the girl's head.

Perhaps the most poignant incident between Paul and myself occurred during the latter part of the school year. One day on returning from the playground to the room, I found that Paul was missing. I looked for him and found him in the hallway. He had moved over a bench to climb upon the windowsill and then had opened the window to look down into the courtyard three stories below.

I asked him to come down from the sill. He refused. I asked him again, and when he refused a second time, I had to lift him bodily from the sill. He thereupon became furious and struck out with both fists and feet, screaming, "I can take care of myself; I don't need you!" I tried to calm him by telling him, "I only took you down so you wouldn't hurt yourself." When he tried to kick me again, crying, "Nothing can hurt me!" I said, "I did it because I like you." He started to strike me again, then suddenly stopped, burst into sobs, and collapsed in my arms. He sobbed for a long time, during which I said nothing, letting him relieve himself of the strong feelings within him.

There was no more said about this incident, but this outbreak of an emotion which Paul had never before, to my knowledge, permitted himself to express and which he had so carefully concealed by stoicism and attempted feats of exaggerated bravery, had finally enabled him to express a side of his personality that was natural in a child of his age. A hint that there existed in Paul a wish to be able to acknowledge sadness, fear, or incapability of certain acts beyond his age and powers, had already been given us in the story he had invented: along with the "ferocious warrior" who wishfully vanquishes giants, there was also the little fox who is afraid that the warrior had gotten hurt and is free to show his feelings by crying "so hard that even his feet got wet."

Summary:

We can gather that Paul had fixed in his mind an image of the male figure which encompassed many of the traits of the traditional unflinching, tight-mouthed adventure-tale hero. (Obviously Paul had not yet discovered Homer's hero, Ulysses, who, by contrast, while capable of the greatest feats in war was given to the longest and loudest wailings in history.) Part of this image of Paul's was due to his father's encouraging him toward an independence beyond his years and his training him in excessive stoicism to "harden the child's character."

Paul had not previously had much opportunity to modify

this concept by association with another person of the male sex who might not hold the same limited view of the role of men. This made for a one-sided picture of the male which, among other things excluded a show of feelings. A display of emotion constituted for Paul a threat to the carefully constructed series of defense-mechanisms against very natural and powerful emotions which Paul felt he must repress.

When, however, Paul had been exposed to a situation in which he saw other children frequently manifest their feelings, and, particularly, when he noted that I, a man, exhibited affection, concern, and at times admitted to not knowing and not being able to do everything, when he found himself in an environment in which it was permissible and not shameful to show fear, sadness, or incapability, he began to find it possible to express those feelings which he had formerly had to repress. He began, in fact, to express them in his conscious behavior, whereas formerly he could only allow himself to express them through inventing a minor character in a story (the fox) or in secretly kind treatment of an animal, or in protection of a much smaller child. It is certainly a reasonable inference that my presence in Paul's school environment contributed measurably toward his development of a more balanced view of the male role.

TOPICS FOR DISCUSSION

Chapter 4 *Paul*

1. Is the average male child of Paul's age supposed to be somewhat of a "stoic" among his peers? Do girls have to be stoics? What factors in our society might contribute to stoicism? How do various national groups differ in regard to this concept?

2. How might a child respond to parental expectations which are too great for him?
3. Are boys in our culture more aggressive than girls? How do girls tend to handle their hostilities?
4. How can hostility be channeled constructively?
5. Who are the heroes in our society? How have they changed in character from those of 50 years ago?

Case 3
George:
"Mother's Boy"

BACKGROUND: *George: aged 5.2 years at entrance; average in-*
telligence; mother 33, housewife; father 39, office
employee; one younger brother 2.6 years; George
had had one year of previous nursery school ex-
perience; general good health, but slight condi-
tion of myopia, corrected by glasses.

George was first brought to school by his father, who stayed
only a few moments since he was on his way to work.
Before leaving, he remarked to George, "Play nice, now.
Mother will call for you this afternoon. And you want her
to hear that you've been good, don't you?" George answered simply, "I want you to stay here." His father said,
"I'd like to stay and watch you play, but I'd get in trouble
with my boss if I were late." He patted George on the head,
turned to me somewhat apologetically and asked, "Do you
think it's all right for me to leave now?"

During the early weeks of the school year, George showed

himself to be cautious; he followed routines closely, and took no initiative in activities. He confined himself to quiet games and spent much of his time in the company of girls, making collages, stringing beads, or working on puzzles.

He avoided the more active outdoor play and took a passive role in his relationship with the boys. In a dramatic play episode dealing with farm life, for example, George drew the haywagon, making believe that he was the horse. He let himself be told when to stop and go and how fast to trot; and he was given his "oats" only after he had obeyed the orders given by the boy who drove the cart. He remained the "horse" during the entire game and did not attempt to take the part of the driver. In another instance, it was George who fetched the blocks for one of the other boys who wanted to construct a garage. In the actual building of the garage, the other children did not include him, nor did he attempt to include himself, but watched passively while they played.

In the woodshop, he often lent his tools freely to another boy and then was too timid to ask the child to return them to him when he needed them himself. He would wait until I encouraged him to ask to have his tools returned.

If he wished to attract the other boys' attention, he felt it necessary to act in such a way as to make himself an object of laughter. For example, the boys were in the dramatic play area one day dressed in home-made cowboy costumes. Using kitchen chairs for horses and ropes tied to the chairs for reins, they were rounding up imaginary cattle to put them in the stables. Some vanquished the invisible bulls with great skill, managing to lasso them and drag them into the stable. The girls in the kitchen were preparing clay pancakes for the hungry cowhands.

George, who had been playing with the girls, at this moment decided to join the boy's game. They paid little attention to him when he got on a chair and started to ride the way they did. He imitated closely the gestures and actions of the other cowboys. When this did not arouse any response from them, George called out in a high, tremulous voice: "I'm falling off my horse! This wild bronco is too much for me!" He pretended that he was slipping from the "horse" and made faces of simulated torment. He went on to act out all the predicaments of an unskilled rider and called loudly for help. One boy cried, "Hold on to the tail of the horse! It's your only chance!" Pretending that he could not find the horse's tail, even though he looked for it on all sides of its body, George tumbled, laughing, to the floor. The others laughed also and seemed to enjoy the spectacle. George tried to get up, then pretended that the horse had pushed him down again and staggered around the "corral." He continued these antics until the children lost interest in what he was doing and went back to "rounding up the bulls." Apparently discouraged, George returned to playing with the girls.

In his behavior toward me, George showed attentiveness and compliance with my wishes. If, for example, I asked the group to move from one area to another for a change of activity, George was invariably the first to do so. He went even further, asking my permission for his going to the toilet or taking a second sheet of drawing paper, matters for which no permission was required. Yet I noticed that George would not turn to me at those times when he needed immediate personal help or assistance, such as when he suffered a slight cut, or wanted a second helping of food or a blanket to cover him at rest hour.

In such cases, he turned exclusively to the woman teacher. His attitude toward her was mixed. Whenever an immediate personal need arose, he went to her in a natural manner, as if he expected her to take care of him, which of course she did. I noticed, however, that whenever she was in complete charge of an activity and I remained in the background or attended to other work, George seemed restless and often vexed. He would sometimes challenge her decisions and balk when asked to do something.

One day, for example, while she was making paper puppets with the children and I was busy elsewhere, George showed signs of being unable to concentrate on his work. Suddenly he threw down the puppet he had been making. The teacher, who happened to be sitting close to him, said, "Is there something wrong? Do you want me to help you with your puppet?" George got up from his chair, pushed his work away and answered angrily, "You think you know everything. Well, you just leave me alone." Before the teacher had a chance to reply, he was gone. He stood looking moodily out of the window. However, a minute later, he returned to the table and asked her to turn up the sleeves of his shirt because he was too warm.

In his play with the girls, George was more assertive than with the boys. He often tried to domineer over them and reacted strongly to any girl who tried to assert her will against his. When there was no conflict about leadership, George was relaxed and seemed to enjoy the games. He knew how to arouse the girls' interest and often invented games to this end, insisting however on playing the central role himself. When this supremacy was challenged, he usually withdrew.

One day, for example, George arranged the dramatic play area to resemble a beauty parlor. He lined the girls up in chairs and proceeded to curl their hair around clothes-pins. On one girl's head, he placed a large casserole, much to her dismay. When she objected, he declared sternly, "That's what you have to do if you want a good permanent wave." The others laughed. One of the girls, whose finger-nails George was covering with red paint, complained, "I don't like the way you are smearing my fingers. You don't know how to do it. Here, let me." And she grabbed the paint brush from his hand. George objected, insisting, "I do so. My mother paints her fingernails all the time. And I saw them do it in the beauty parlor, too. Give me back that brush." The girl held the brush behind her back, and when he tried to reach it, she pushed him away. He left the area angrily and did not return. When I saw him a few moments later, he had gone to an easel and started a painting. He painted with quick strokes and, soon becoming impatient, tore the first piece of paper from the easel, started a second time, then became dissatisfied again and crumpling the sheet of paper, threw it on the floor.

So it was that during the early part of the school year George showed ambivalent feelings in many areas of his behavior. In his relationship with the boys, he exhibited an eagerness and willingness to play; but, apparently uncertain whether they would accept him, he resorted to either pas-sively following or becoming subservient to them. Alter-natively, he would attempt to attract their attention and approval by clowning, as in his portrayal of an unskillful cowboy. But when after a time their interest lagged, he would return to playing with the girls.

He was assertive and independent, on the other hand, in his behavior with the girls, often showing a desire to dominate them. He appeared to use them to test his strength and employed games that aroused their interest to make himself the center of their attention. He was more successful in achieving this dominance with the girls than with the boys. If, however, his dominant position were challenged, he struggled to keep it, as he did not among the boys. When thwarted by a display of greater power on the part of a girl, he retreated from the scene. That his experience was a disturbing one to him can be seen, for example, in his inability to concentrate on his painting after his defeat in the "beauty parlor."

In his reactions to me, George showed himself compliant and in need of my approbation. Yet, though he came to consult me in matters of accepted routine, he showed that he felt unable to turn to me for the fulfillment of his immediate personal needs. He did not express his wishes or desires to me, and, in consequence, his rapport with me was limited.

With the woman teacher, George showed greater freedom, both in expecting her to take care of his immediate needs and in expressing his feelings to her. He did, however, show signs of hostility when she was in a dominant position in the group; at those times he tended to resent her offers of help, apparently interpreting them, as in the puppet incident, as attempts to dominate him. Since, however, he seemed to have felt also that he had to rely on her for help, he alternated between feelings of rebellion and dependence.

We can thus see George's concept of the male role in relation to women: It is a dependent one, George's behavior alternates between attempts to rebel against being dominated and to avoid such domination by himself assuming a dominant role. If however he is thwarted in this respect, he either returns to a dependent role or shows disturbance.

These aspects of George's behavior were further clarified by a conference I had with his mother a short time later. Speaking of him as "little Georgie," she complained that he had refused to tell her about his school activities. This she found very surprising, since, as she said, her boy and she had always been "so close." There was nothing he had ever "hidden" from her.

She went on to say that she had always "shouldered the entire burden" of her children's upbringing. In speaking of her husband, she declared that he liked the children, but that he was in "delicate health" and she did not like to bother him with their little everyday problems; in any case she, as the mother, knew best how to deal with these. When I asked her how much time her husband was able to spend with the children, she said that on weekends he often played with them or took them to see their relatives, if he was not "too tired."

Some time later, George told a story in school which threw further light on his conception of the respective functions of parents in family life. A small group of children were seated on the floor and George offered to tell them a story. They asked for "Goldilocks and the Three Bears." He began to tell this story in the traditional way, but soon the narrative changed and evolved in the direction of George's own ideas.

Three small bears lived in a cave with their mother and

father. One Sunday they decided to go on a picnic, but the mother bear went to see her grandmother, who had the measles. So the three small bears and their father went out to look for honey. They saw a bee with a belly full of honey. They followed him and soon came to a big beehive. They tried to get some honey, but the bees got angry and chased them away. They chased the bears all the way down to the river so that they had to jump in. When they got out, they shook themselves like dogs and got dry in the sun. Then they looked around for something to eat, because they were very hungry. They saw a big apple orchard with lots of trees. That was just what they liked. They gobbled up all the apples they could. The father bear ate so much that he got sleepy. He lay down under a tree and was soon asleep. The small bears weren't tired, so they played ball with one of the apples. One time the apple rolled so far that they had to go and look for it in the woods. They didn't know how to get back. So they were lost. And it got dark and they started to cry, but nobody came. Then all of a sudden they saw a flashlight behind the trees. It was the mother bear. She took them by the back of the neck and scolded them. Then she took them home.

When George had ended the story, one of the children asked, "And what happened to the father bear?" George answered, "Oh, he got home late and his dinner was all cold."

In this story, we see the father depicted as occupying a status equal to that of his three children. He goes looking for honey with them, is chased by the bees, jumps in the river, and gorges himself with apples, just as they do. He does not exert any authority, nor assume any role of leadership. He does not contribute to the protection of his children; instead, he falls asleep as soon as the opportunity presents itself, leaving the three children to their own devices. When they get lost and cry for help, he does not appear, nor is he heard of again in the story after he falls asleep. To the question of what happened to the father bear, George's answer indicates that the father is in a sense punished by having his dinner get cold. Since it is the role of the mother to prepare dinner, it can be assumed that it is she who metes out this punishment.

The mother, on the other hand, is given a responsible role from the very beginning of the story when she goes to take care of the grandmother sick with the measles. She appears again at the end of the story when she is most needed, disciplines the children, yet takes care of them by bringing them to their home. It is not until George is asked a question by another child that he concerns himself with the sleeping father at all.

We have seen that George's mother herself sees her role as one of superior responsibility; she claims closer contact with her children and assigns to her husband a minor role in their upbringing. In the story, which represents George's point of view on these matters, the father bear plays an important part in providing entertainment for his children and joining in their adventures. At no point, however, is he given an authoritative part in the action of the story, nor does he make any attempt to guide his children. The climax of the story indicates the dominant place of the mother: it is she who metes out discipline to the children and, in some measure, to the father himself.

These attitudes would seem to be consistent with George's behavior in the classroom. He showed very little if any tendency to rely on me in case of immediate need. He expected this help from the woman teacher, yet when she was in a dominant position he felt the same resentment towards her, as, it can be assumed, he also felt towards his mother. This resentment, which was probably also a wish for greater independence, was sensed by his mother, who complained that George refused to tell her of his school activities. George's attitude of rebellion is ambivalently coupled with a strong need for dependence and a desire to be taken care of. Since the infrequent presence of his father seldom permitted George to turn to him, he had of necessity to turn mainly to his mother for the gratification of these needs.

Toward the latter part of the school year, a gradual change developed in George's behavior pattern. His relationship with the boys became somewhat more secure. He participated in more of the active physical games, included himself more freely in the group, and no longer seemed to feel that he had to play a subservient role to be accepted. In a game of human trains, for example, in which the children lined up one behind the other, George insisted on being the "locomotive" when his turn came, whereas before he would have contented himself with being the "last car." So, too, in the construction of an elaborate sand castle he participated equally with another boy in getting the water and wielding the necessary tools. Nor was George any longer the first to follow obediently the routines of the day. Instead he did his share of lagging behind and objecting to things he did not wish to do.

He was now somewhat more ready to turn to me for help, if I were available, instead of always to the woman teacher. He would let me take a splinter from his hand, or ask me to divide the candy which he had brought to school to be shared by the children. At other times, when he felt fright or elation, he began to show more readiness to come to me for reassurance or simply out of the desire to express his feelings to me. His rapport with me improved considerably.

He began to exhibit less dependence on the woman teacher and also less resentment toward her. Through practical experience and careful guidance, he came to see that she and I shared the responsibility of the children's care. He thus began to realize that when she was in sole charge of the group, it did not mean that she intended to impose her will upon him.

Some change also took place in George's behavior toward the girls. He was still assertive in his relations with them, but he tended to dominate them less and to be not quite so concerned about maintaining the status of a dominant figure among them, nor was he as upset as formerly if another child assumed that position.

Summary:

The case of George reveals another of the effects of infrequent participation of the father in the upbringing of the young child. In this instance, the effects were heightened by the dominant nature of the mother and her tendency to minimize the responsibilities connected with the father's role. Hence both the mother and the child himself placed little emphasis upon the functions of the father. The structure of George's family circle, moreover, provided him with limited opportunities for a realistic and all-inclusive interpretation of the male figure. George's identification with the masculine figure was underdeveloped for a child of his age. It is therefore not surprising to note in him an uncertainty in his behavior toward both boys and men, together with an unclear concept of his own role as a boy.

Through consistent everyday contact with adults of both sexes, and by being placed in an environment conducive to constructive realizations, George was furnished with a great number and variety of opportunities to qualify and modify his concepts of the separate roles of men and women. He was thus enabled to understand better his role as a boy and a boy's relation to adults and to his peers. As he grew more confident of his place among boys, and as his concept of the male role became clearer, his relationships with all concerned showed general improvement.

TOPICS FOR DISCUSSION

Chapter 5 *George*
1. Has the changing role of women contributed to making men less masculine?
2. What are some of the factors which may contribute to the development of deviant sexual patterns?
3. How might giving greater importance of the father's role contribute to normal psycho-sexual development in the child?
4. Are the roles that men and women portray more or less differentiated now than 50 years ago?
5. What might be some of the effects of a family situation in which the mother is an extremely dominant person and the father is a docile, unassertive individual?

Case 4
Barbara:
In Her Mother's Image

BACKGROUND: *Barbara: 4.9 years at entrance; high intelligence; mother 35, not working; father 40, business man; only child; no previous nursery school experience; normal birth, bottle-fed; excellent physical condition.*

Barbara came into the room on the first day of school, introduced herself rather formally to me, and asked my name. Her mother remained in the hall-way in case Barbara needed her. The child went to the hall several times to reassure herself that she was still there.

During the first weeks, Barbara played mostly by herself. She drew with crayons (but did not paint), looked at books, and examined the dolls; she refused to participate in clay modeling, collage work, or sand constructions, saying, "I don't like those dirty games." She also avoided those activities which required physical dexterity and some daring, such as the use of the climbing apparatus, the sliding-pond, and the seesaws, although she had good coordination and more than adequate muscular development. When asked by the other children to join in these games, she would say, "It's dizzy up there," or "My dress is too short." When on one occasion, another girl answered, "My dress is just as short and I always climb," Barbara said to her, "My mother doesn't like me to."

In one dramatic play episode, Barbara and another girl were playing "house." Barbara, having covered her dress with a large apron, swept the floor, commenting the while on how dirty it was. The other child asked her to help make the food for the "baby." The "food," consisting of sawdust, flour, and water, was being kneaded by the girl with her hands. Barbara refused to help roll out the "bread," saying, "I'd rather prepare the plates and set the table." When the bread was baked, they both got the doll and placed her in a chair. Barbara put a bib around her neck. Just as the other girl was about to put a spoonful of food to the doll's mouth, Barbara said hurriedly: "Wait a minute. You can't let her eat like this. Just look at those hands. She's filthy. What a bad baby!" She ran to get a washcloth and scrubbed the doll's face and hands until they were immaculately clean.

Another day, Barbara and three other girls were listening to records in a corner of the room. They decided to dance to the music. Barbara seemed a little hesitant at first, but soon joined the others in twirling about, skipping, and holding her skirt "the way ballerinas do." One of the girls had put on high heels and the others had taken their shoes off. A boy who happened to be playing close by came over to watch them dance. Then he sat down next to the phonograph and began to observe the record spinning around. As soon as Barbara noticed him, she stopped dancing and said in a loud whisper to one of the girls: "Stop dancing. Quick, or he'll see your panties!" The girl paid no attention to her warning, however, and continued dancing with complete unconcern. Barbara seemed puzzled and sat down without speaking.

A somewhat similar attitude was noted at another time, and in an even more revealing manner. All the children in the group freely used the same bathroom, which included wash basins and toilets, and it was customary for them to go to the toilet if they had to, during intervals after mealtime or before the rest hour. I began to notice that Barbara always lagged behind the others; in fact, she repeatedly remained in the hallway, waiting until all the other children had left the bathroom. Once I overhead another girl who saw her there ask, "Why don't you ever come in when we're here?" Barbara answered, "I don't like it when the boys are there." The other child seemed surprised. "Why?" Barbara hesitated, then answered, "Because it's not nice."

It was an accepted practice in our group, approved by the parents, that natural functions and body differences between boys and girls should be treated casually and as a normal part of experience.

A conference with Barbara's mother disclosed some of her attitudes on the upbringing of the child. She seemed overly concerned with matters of cleanliness, health, and safety. Was the climbing apparatus, she asked me at one point, strong enough to support the wear and tear of the children's use? When I assured her that we took the utmost precautions for the children's safety, she said: "You may think that I worry too much about these things. My husband thinks I do. He'd like Barbara to be brought up with as much freedom as he had when he was a child. But a boy is different." She paused, then went on, "When you have a girl, you just can't be too careful."

As we have noted, Barbara displayed reticence and a tendency to avoid any sort of play, such as climbing, in which she thought there might be some physical danger. But this reticence was not based solely on the fear of physical danger; it also involved the wish to avoid showing certain portions of her body and the consciousness that her mother did not like her to engage in such activities. Barbara showed signs of repugnance toward play which entailed the use of material, such as paint, clay, glue, and sand, which might soil her clothes or hands. In addition, she exhibited the wish to avoid being seen or seeing other children, especially those of the opposite sex, in circumstances, such as dancing or attending to bodily functions, which might involve the risk of exposing certain parts of the anatomy.

The presence of these attitudes was corroborated by the worried remarks of the child's mother during her interview with me about the dangers of various sorts from which a child of the female sex had to be protected. Such excessive concern entered into inhibiting the child's natural desire to explore her social and physical environment.

Judging from the remark made by Barbara's mother concerning her husband's more expansive and less fearful conception of the upbringing of a child, we may assume that were the child to have had more frequent contact with the father, there would have been more opportunity for her to develop a less limiting approach to the world around her. This assumption is strengthened by changes in Barbara's behavior which took place at about the middle of the school year.

At that time, Barbara evinced a growing interest in those

areas of experience which she had formerly tended to
avoid. A conflict was observed, for example, between her
desire, on the one hand, to avoid participation in a game
which involved walking over a narrow plank placed on two
blocks of wood, and, on the other, her obvious fascination
for the game. Three children were playing "Ships." The
captain called, "All aboard, we're leaving for Africa." The
other two "sailors" hurried over the gang-plank, but Barbara
would not cross it; she remained on the shore waving to
them as they sailed away. It was not until the other children
were safely out of the way, somewhere deep in "Africa,"
that she hesitatingly looked at the plank, then lowered both
of its ends to the ground. She tried to walk over it without
losing her balance. When she had succeeded in doing this
several times, she then proceeded to put one end of the
plank up on the block of wood, and walked up the slight
incline slowly. When she had completed this feat, she
seemed pleased and jumped off the end of the plank with
great nonchalance.

During clay work, Barbara set with the other children,
but would not at first touch the material before her. She
did, however, begin to express her interest by asking several
children what they were making and whether they would
take their work home when it was finished. After several
days of this, she finally took some wooden sticks and began
to manipulate the clay in the following manner: she hit
the clay until it was softened and flattened, then folded over
the ends, and finally achieved a textural pattern by digging
the ends of the sticks into the surface of the material. She
did not at any time touch the clay with her hands. When
one of the children said to her, "That's nice. What is it?"
Barbara answered, "It's a turtle." Whereupon the first

child said, "I don't see the head or the tail." Barbara thought for a moment. "He's not showing them. He's asleep." When another child commented, "Tomorrow it will be time to paint it and then you can take it home," Barbara answered quickly, "No, it's too messy to take home."

She showed the same interest and concern, mixed with hesitancy and avoidance, on several occasions when sex-differences between boys and girls or between animals were discussed. One day I had taken the entire group to the nature room to see a litter of rabbits born a few days before. The mother rabbit was in her cage, nursing the small animals. "When they're babies like that, they're always hungry," one of the children observed. Another asked, "What are they doing, biting the mother?" To which still another child answered, "No. They don't have any teeth. They're drinking the milk that comes out of the mother." They all crowded around to look. Then one child asked, "Where's the father rabbit?" "He probably went to the movies," another suggested. Everyone laughed.

During this conversation, Barbara had remained behind the other children and had not wished to come near the cage. She listened attentively, however, to what was being said. Suddenly, one of the boys called, "I bet this is the father," and he pointed to a large rabbit in another cage. "How do you know?" one child asked, "he looks just like the other rabbit." Someone else suggested, "Because he hasn't got any babies." "Oh no, that's not how you know," the first boy replied, "you have to turn him over on his back and look if you really want to be sure."

When the children asked me whether they might look at the rabbit in question to find out whether it was male or female, Barbara came to me and said, "I don't like it here.

It smells. Let's go back to our room." The rest of the children disagreed loudly, and Barbara went to another part of the nature room, where our conversation could not be overheard and from where the rabbit was not visible. When I looked in her direction a few moments later, I saw that she was crouched on the floor before the aquarium and was looking closely at the undersides of the fish.

Barbara's behavior patterns indicated attitudinal conflicts in three important areas of experience; participation in games involving physical prowess; play with materials which might soil the hands or clothes; discussions or actions that concern sex-differences or anatomy. Although reticence, fear, or repugnance were Barbara's initial reactions in these areas, there existed in her also the opposite drive, for she expressed interest, curiosity, and a desire to experiment in these "forbidden" areas of experience. She felt it necessary, however, to resort to indirect or compensatory mechanisms to satisfy her desire for exploration of these areas. The use of an indirect or compensatory mechanism can be seen at work in her lowering of the "ship's plank" to the ground in order to walk on it without having to risk its dangers and in the use of sticks to manipulate the clay in order not to have to touch the material with her hands. It is significant that her choice of subject matter should be a turtle with its body extremities hidden from view. The animal is further removed from actual contact with the outside world by being asleep. It is further significant that, although she had been able to bring herself to work with the clay which she formerly considered "dirty," Barbara was not willing to go so far as to bring the finished product home. Her retreat from the area of direct exploration of the sex-differences of the rabbits to the less direct examination of the undersides of fish behind the glass walls of the aquarium was yet another defense mechanism.

As noted, a gradual change had begun to take place in Barbara. She became more willing to explore those areas which she had formerly avoided entirely. She had begun to desire a fuller participation in the life around her. Her use of indirect or compensatory mechanisms to achieve these ends enabled her to cope with a conflict of desires, helping to reduce it to a manageable form. Barbara was not yet certain enough of her own strength to be able to face and resolve these conflicts directly.

An incident which took place toward the latter part of the school year further illustrated the direction of Barbara's development and some of the underlying causes for her behavior. The children were making Easter cards by cutting out varicolored papers, pasting bits together, and drawing on them. Many of the children made one card for both parents. Barbara began by making one card also. This she did with extreme care, drawing outlines with the help of a straight piece of wood and limiting herself to the use of two colors. When she had completed this card, she reflected for a moment, then turned to her neighbor and said, "This one is going to be for my mother." And when the other child asked, "And what about your father?" Barbara answered eagerly, "I'm going to make a different one for him." She asked for several more small pieces of colored paper and began to cut and glue them onto a larger sheet. She crayoned the whole freely, making various designs. She even glued some cotton to the center of the card. She then went to one of the easels and proceeded to paint over the crayon drawing. When she brought the card back to the table, the child next to her exclaimed, "That's beautiful!" Someone else said, "But you used too much glue; it's not neat like the other one." Barbara answered, "I know, but my daddy won't mind. He'll like it all right."

It is apparent that Barbara's attitudes toward her parents were projected in her treatment of the particular card destined for each of them. The one made for the mother was a cautious piece of work, with an accent on neatness and conformity; the one made for the father, freer and more venturesome. And in the card intended for her father, Barbara even goes so far as to use glue and paint, two materials which she had formerly avoided, confident that he "will like it all right."

The very act of producing a piece of work for the father seemingly liberated in the child her impulses toward free experimentation with materials formerly taboo to her. Presumably, if the father had had more occasion to participate in the upbringing of the child, these positive impulses would have been strengthened. Presumably also, had the father been able to contribute more frequently to the formation of the child's personality, many of her conflicts would have been non-existent or present in a much milder form. The more frequent presence of the father would have moderated the influence of the mother and given the child a better balanced perspective.

During the entire school year, both the woman teacher and I encouraged Barbara's exploration of those areas of experience with which she was capable of coping at any given time. We did not at any point force her to undertake tasks beyond her powers, preferring to praise and sustain her whenever she attempted to emerge into fuller participation. The interest and social approval of her peers also encouraged further movement in this direction.

When it was noted that, so far as entering into areas of experience to which she had formerly shown reticence was concerned, Barbara was more responsive to suggestions from me, I attempted to guide her slowly in this direction. As she became more confident of her own ability to cope with these situations and as she became better acquainted with the permissive attitude of the woman teacher, she began to feel free to accept similar suggestions from her.

In interviews with the mother, I attempted, by matter-of-fact references to the usual school routines, to point out to her the positive value of exploration and experimentation on the part of children. I suggested also that she come and observe her child in the group activities, in the hope that this would help her to modify some of her own attitudes and permit her to view her daughter more objectively.

By the end of the school year, Barbara was better able to participate directly in those areas where she had formerly shown conflict and consequent use of compensatory mechanisms. She had begun to play on the lowest rungs of the climbing apparatus, would sit on the center of the seesaw to balance it for two other children, had begun to mix the paints herself, and had handled clay without the use of sticks or other intermediaries. Barbara continued to show a preference for going to the bathroom alone, but she did on occasion enter it when other children were present.

Summary:

The study of Barbara illustrates once more the constructive influence the father might have had upon the child had he been able to play a greater part in her upbringing and thus been able to modify the mother's restricted view of child rearing. Instead, the greater part of the child's behavior was influenced by the attitudes of the mother. The restrictive nature of these attitudes was reflected in Barbara's inability to participate in activities not sanctioned by the mother. The mother's opinions were further strengthened by the child's infrequent exposure to the contrasting views of the father. Thus, there resulted a limited acquaintance and confidence on the part of Barbara in those areas of experience in which the father's personality might have encouraged and sustained her.

Barbara did partially resolve some of the conflicts which prevented her from realizing her full potentialities. The improvement noted was very gradual, and, to my knowledge, was not achieved by any change in the home environment. The definite signs of progress can be attributed principally to the advantage of her close and continued contact with adults of both sexes.

TOPICS FOR DISCUSSION

Chapter 6 *Barbara*

1. How are parental attitudes toward sex communicated to children?
2. When should sex-education begin? Who should be responsible for educating the child concerning the "facts of life"?
3. How might the quality of the relationship that exists between parents affect the child's psycho-sexual development?
4. In what way is the child's attitude toward and expression of sex molded by (a) the peer group? (b) the school? (c) the community? (d) the culture?

5. What aids to proper sex-education are generally available today for children, parents, and teachers?
6. How might the personality of a teacher reflect constructive or destructive attitudes towards sex?

PART III

CHILDREN IN FATHERLESS HOMES

Case 5

Harriet:

A Quest for the Past

BACKGROUND: *Harriet: age 4.10 years at entrance; mother 32, secretary; father 39, in military service; child's parents divorced 6 months before; child in custody of the mother, often cared for by woman neighbor; no other children; seldom sees father; same residence for mother and child as before divorce; child has had 1 year previous nursery school experience. Average intelligence; normal birth, bottle-fed; good physical condition.*

When Harriet first entered the group, her mother remained with her for a few minutes and showed her some toys she was familiar with or which were similar to those she had used in her last year's nursery school class. "You ought to feel right at home here," the mother remarked. Then she turned to me, declaring that she would have to leave for work right away, since she had some important papers to finish at her office. When I asked her whether Harriet was prepared to have her leave so soon, she answered: "Oh, she's used to this. She has to learn to take care of herself." Whereupon she gave the child a quick kiss and departed.

Harriet did not seem as able to take care of herself as her mother apparently liked to think. She was on the verge of tears during the entire day, but she managed to occupy herself with dolls and talk to some of the children. She seemed to take some comfort from the fact that she was more familiar with the physical environment than were the others. She spent most of the day arranging the dramatic play area, putting the doll clothes and dishes in order, and conversing occasionally with children near her. Although she was generally amiable enough with them, she seemed critical of their actions. She admonished several girls who were also active in the dramatic play area, saying, for instance: "That's not how you make a doll's bed. You have to make the pillow neat," or, "I wonder who messed up all those dishes. This house looks like there was a fire in it."

Harriet's preoccupation with order displayed itself constantly. One day she and another girl were washing some of the doll clothing and hanging it up to dry. The other child hung the clothes somewhat haphazardly, fixing them with clothes-pins as best she could. Harriet watched her with apparent dissatisfaction, and when the girl was finished, she proceeded to re-arrange all the clothes in a neat line, grumbling to herself while doing so. When she had completed her task, she said with a sigh of relief; "That's better. Now this house is all fixed up. It makes me dizzy when everything is jumbled."

Another time, standing next to the easel of one of the girls, Harriet noticed the painting the child had almost finished. The picture was one of a garden with flowers growing in it. Harriet commented immediately; "Your flowers are all mixed up. I can't even tell one from the other." The girl replied: "I know their names. And I like it this way." Harriet thought for a moment, then said, "I'm going to paint a garden too. Watch me!" She commenced to paint a very few flowers growing straight up from a flat plane of green and separated from each other by dark vertical lines. When the girl next to her said, "Oh you put up a fence," Harriet replied: "Those are sticks. And every flower has its name written on the stick." When the girl asked, "Why is that?" Harriet answered, "It has to be. So you know where to find them."

This passion for order manifested itself mainly in connection with inanimate objects which she could control, and in situations in which she was in a somewhat dominant position. For the most part, also, this behavior occurred when another girl was her playmate. In such cases, Harriet made attempts to influence the other child, to impose her sense of order, or she would find the other's work inadequate.

Her behavior changed when she was in the company of boys or when her playmates included both boys and girls. She seemed at first somewhat stunned by the presence of the boys, said and did very little when boys were in the group, or watched without joining the game. Later, when she did participate, she seemed very eager to please the boys and to have them accept her. At these times, she appeared ready to give up her preoccupation with order, at least temporarily, if the boys chose to attribute little importance to this factor, but she remained very critical toward the girls if they did the same.

Once, two of the boys asked Harriet and another girl to have a tug-of-war with them. Harriet offered to find a piece of rope for the purpose. She and one of the boys looked everywhere in the drawers of the kitchen cabinet in search of a clothesline, scattering objects all over the floor in the process. Harriet, oblivious of the disorder they were creating, exclaimed excitedly: "Here it is! I got the rope!" For the actual tug-of-war, one boy and one girl competed at a time, pulling at either end of the rope with all their might until one had overcome the other. When it was Harriet's turn, she laughed a great deal and pretended to pull with all her strength; but although she was obviously bigger and more powerful than the boy who was her opponent, she allowed him to win.

When the game no longer interested the children and the boys wandered away, the other girl suggested that she and Harriet try out the new crayons we had gotten that day. Harriet loved to draw, but she answered, "No. I can't. Just look at the kitchen floor!" And when the other child replied, "Who cares?" Harriet grew quite angry and remarked, "I care. And the dolls do too. They're sitting there all alone. And they don't even know where they are, the house looks so different."

Harriet's behavior revealed that she had a strong need to reassure herself and to gain some control over her feelings and the outside world by giving to inanimate objects a sense of order. She expressed on various occasions some of the reasons underlying this need.

Note especially her remark concerning the feelings of the dolls. The child's own personal feelings are in this instance projected directly into the dolls, and she is expressing, through them, her sense of confusion and isolation, as well as her fear of being stranded in unknown or unfamiliar surroundings. The surroundings can be made tangible and recognizable only if a strict and habitual pattern is established among the inanimate objects. The concern for order indicates fear of disorder. Her statements show that she connects disorder with disruption of the home, where the persons involved in this disruption "don't even know where they are."

Harriet is seen to be struggling against the disruption of her own home (that is, against the recent divorce of her parents) and she is attempting to regain a semblance of order, or at least to safeguard the few remaining reassuring aspects of her life by imposing a pattern known to her upon any situation which appears chaotic. A compensatory mechanism is at work once again: the child is attempting to construct order on a smaller and less challenging scale than that represented by the actual disruption of her home, which is beyond her power to control or rectify. No pleasure comes from this activity; it merely serves to appease to some extent her desperate need to cling to some reassuring pattern vaguely connected with the home she knew before it was broken by divorce.

This compensatory behavior manifested itself mainly when Harriet was in the company of girls. It was temporarily abandoned when she played with boys. Quite probably, her need for male attention was strong enough to mitigate her other concern. Her desire for the attention of the boys was illustrated not only in her ability to discard her preoccupation with order, but also in her willingness to play a somewhat passive role to please them. Thus, she permitted an obviously weaker boy to win the tug-of-war. As soon as the game was over, however, she returned to putting her "house" in order.

In Harriet's reactions to adults, two sets of attitudes may

be observed. With the woman teacher, she showed evidence of a strong need for affection and reassurance. At times, she exhibited a desire to be physically comforted, to be held or to have her head stroked, especially at rest hour or when she was very tired. She made efforts to be demonstrative and helpful: for example, she offered to help set the lunch table whenever the woman teacher was in charge and she liked to walk next to her when we were going to the playground. She also showed that she wished to be protected and aided by her when she was in difficulties with another child or had a problem with an unfamiliar activity.

Towards me, Harriet was more reticent. Her behavior with me consisted mainly of ascertaining my approval or disapproval of her actions and of expressing concern over whether she was succeeding in pleasing me. She went to the extent of asking me many times a day whether she had "done anything wrong," or whether I "wasn't maybe angry with her." When I reassured her, and asked later why she supposed I would be angry or would think she had done anything wrong, she hesitated and then answered, "Because I want to know if you like me."

This attitude was manifested at other times also. One day, when Harriet was watering the flowers she accidentally knocked over one of the tin containers in which they grew, and the dirt spilled onto the floor. As I happened to be near, I came over to her. Before I had a chance to say anything, she had begun to cry and was frantically picking up the bits of earth to put them back into the pot. She looked up at me and said, "I spoiled it. Look, the stem's all crooked." Although I assured her that we could fix the plant, she cried even harder and said, "You're mad at me, I know, because I'm always breaking things." When I had succeeded in calming her somewhat, she began to sweep up every grain of earth and then rearranged all the flowerpots on the windowsill so that they stood in a neat row. She appeared relieved when she had done all this, put the broom away, and said, "That's better. Now it looks almost like before."

At about this time, I had a conference with Harriet's mother. After asking me general questions about the girl's adjustment in school, she began to mention that she was puzzled and somewhat worried about Harriet's behavior at home. She was very moody, cried easily, and had lately begun to insist on not having her room painted; earlier she had refused to have any changes made in its furnishings. Harriet's mother asked whether the child spoke a good deal about her father in school, since at home she was constantly asking about him and wanting to know where he was and what he was doing at various times of the day. She went on to say that Harriet saw her father only once every few months, when he was on leave in the city for a few days. At these times, the mother remarked, "He takes the child to all sorts of places. Naturally she gets all excited and can't wait until she sees him again." After these visits, Harriet usually seemed upset, frequently wanted to know whether her mother thought that "daddy will come back again," and would ask with reference to all her daily activities, "Would daddy like me to do this?"

Harriet's preoccupation with making some sort of contact with her father manifested itself in school, also. I noticed that she listened intently whenever other children talked about their fathers, and whenever reference was made to a father in a story, or to father-animals, or even to toy figures portraying men. One day, upon seeing another child make a birthday present for his father, she got a large

piece of paper and several crayons, remarking, "I'm going
to write a letter to my daddy." One of the children who had
overheard her said, "You know how to write? I won't know
till next year." "Sure I know," Harriet replied; "I write
lots of letters." She sat down and proceeded to draw a few
letters of the alphabet and some numbers, alternated with
pictures of children, houses, and various designs in color.
The child who had spoken to her before watched fascinated
by the process. Then she said, "But that's not a letter. A
letter reads." Harriet answered, "Mine reads. I'll tell you
what it says." She pointed to the right side of the page: "It
starts here. Dear daddy. . . . I miss you. . . . Where are you
now? . . . Do you live in a house?" The other child
laughed. "Sure he lives in a house. Everybody does." Harriet answered: "Not my daddy. He's different. Sometimes he
lives in a boat and sometimes he lives in a plane. And he
goes far away." Then she added, "My mother told me that."

Harriet began to show greater attachment to me than
before. She seemed to have somewhat less need to reassure
herself that her every action pleased me or that she had not
done anything to alienate me. But when the slightest conflict involving this need arose, she became very upset. She
was brought to school late one day and when she arrived
I had already gone out with a group of children to purchase
supplies for a party. On my return I found Harriet in tears.
At first she refused to talk to me, but when I told her that
we had been looking for her because we had wanted her to
go shopping with us, she said, "It's because I couldn't find
my socks this morning. And I always put them in the same
place, in my shoes. But today they weren't there. So you
went away without me."

I told her that she could go with me to get supplies the

next time, adding that anybody could misplace his socks. But she did not appear to be comforted by my words. The incident had apparently disturbed her the entire day, for on leaving she asked me anxiously, "Will you be here tomorrow morning, if I come on time?" "You know I'm always here," I answered, "unless I'm not feeling well, and that only happens once in a long time." She looked more reassured after my answer, but she was obviously relieved the next morning to find me really there as usual when she came in the door.

A correlation existed, as we can note from the preceding incidents, between Harriet's behavior at home and in school. Her mother was apparently rather matter-of-fact in her treatment of the child, expecting her to be able to adjust to reality and to new situations just as she, in all likelihood, had had to do herself. Although she had a fairly good insight into her daughter's problems, she did not, from my observations, give the child all the warmth she was seeking. It is therefore not surprising that Harriet should turn eagerly to the woman teacher for this much-needed affection.

The child not only missed her father, but worried over whether he would return to see her, and whether she had succeeded in pleasing him and had thus assured herself of even his infrequent presence; conversely, she feared that by actions displeasing to him, she might further remove him from her life. It was as if the child considered herself in some measure responsible for the absence of the father, and believed that the preservation of an established order might influence or even effect his return. (As has been noted, she refused to have any changes made in her room which might disrupt the established order there.) Her concern in this respect is echoed in the instance of Harriet's misplacing her socks and then attributing to this fact her exclusion from my presence.

Harriet's extreme preoccupation with order, which indicates a desire to exert an almost magical control over the actions of others, also reflected a feeling that she was somehow responsible for her father's departure. To assuage her guilt, Harriet turned to the same sense of order, which then became a comforting agent, somewhat alleviating the sense of guilt. Such mechanisms, alternately creating and reducing guilt, are of course detrimental in that they perpetuate and continually reformulate the same problem, without allowing a child to deal realistically with it in a real environment. They not only limit the possibility of experimenting with other modes of behavior, but also obstruct the child's vision of her self and of her parents. In other words, as long as Harriet, on the one hand, blamed herself for her father's absence and, on the other, felt that she could magically influence his return, she was not able to find relief from her tensions, nor could she understand her own role or her status in relation to others. She had assigned to herself powers and responsibilities which rightly belong to adults, or which are even beyond the control of adults.

During the latter part of the school year, however, Harriet began to relax somewhat her vigilance in regard to order. Through her school activities and the attitudes of the children around her, she slowly began to become accustomed to the idea that order is only functional and that, in human relationships especially, it is not of primary importance. As incidents arose which gave us the opportunity to strengthen her sense of security in the adults with whom she was in daily contact, we were able to help Harriet develop relationships that were not as fraught with tension as were those in her home. The very predictability of the school environment, the constant and daily repetition of routines and experiences, served to reassure her.

Although no dramatic changes were observed in the child at this period, the direction in which she was proceeding was encouraging. (The very slowness of the process promised to make it a more lasting one; sudden and fundamental changes might have been too upsetting for a child who had already suffered from so many brusque alterations of her life pattern.) There were definite indications progress was taking place. Formerly, she had always kept her locker in meticulous order, to the point of giving up a favorite game in order to arrange and rearrange it to perfection; now she gave it much less attention. Similarly, as she worked with several boys and girls on day on a group mural, she stopped at one point and remarked to her neighbor, "This painting needs some fish. I'm going to paint one right here in this water." She proceeded to do so, placing the fish in a space which she had previously covered with blue paint; then she said, "He needs more water to swim around in." She added more paint, then remarked, "And this is where he is going to live." She drew clumps of grass with quick, irregular strokes, and watched the colors run together. Another day, while Harriet was carrying some water for making soap bubbles, the can slipped from her hands and its contents splashed onto the floor. She hesitated for a moment, then called another girl over to help her wipe it up. They got large rags and were soon laughingly squeezing the water back into the tin can. And when Harriet saw me pass, she called to me, "Look how nice and shiny we've made this floor."

Harriet was clearly beginning to modify some of her rigid behavior patterns in favor of a more natural and expansive use of her environment. She was able to enter into play without so many self-imposed restrictions; and she obtained greater satisfaction from it because she was less fearful of being held responsible if things went wrong. In painting the fish, she did not feel compelled to place the animal in a narrowly restricted space, as she had done with the flowers in an earlier work. The fish are now allowed to venture out beyond the vicinity of the house into a new and unknown domain. They are allowed to move about freely, surrounded with life-giving substance, and are no longer tagged with labels to retain a recognizable order.

Harriet was now becoming better able to work in the company of both boys and girls, she no longer assumed a passive role with boys but maintained an equal position among them. In the incident of the spilled water it was apparent that decided progress had taken place when one compares it to the incident in which some spilled dirt had produced in the child great anxiety and a fear of losing my affection. Now, the spilled water is wiped up with the help of another child. Harriet no longer assumes the entire responsibility of putting things in order. And she is able to make the best of an accident, no longer seeming to fear a consequent loss of my favor. Harriet had begun to share experiences which formerly she would have taken entirely upon herself and also to incorporate in her own behavior some of the attitudes of her teachers and her peers.

Summary:

We found in our observation of Harriet that the divorce of her parents had created manifold emotional tensions.

She suffered from a sense of responsibility for her father's absence and an accompanying feeling of guilt. She also felt that she should somehow be able to prevent his absence from becoming even more frequent. Her excessive recourse to order and her insistence on keeping familiar patterns undisturbed apparently served as a means of creating a state reminiscent of former harmony in the home. She also hoped these mechanisms would control factors beyond her power and alleviate her sense of guilt that it might be her fault that the status quo in the home had been disturbed.[1]

The effects of the child's preoccupation with order were numerous. For one thing, it caused her to exclude from her range of experience many activities and satisfactions. The sense of guilt underlying her preoccupation further limited her conception of her environment and distorted many human relationships; it forced her to interpret the reactions of others in the light of her own anxiety and sense of guilt. Finally, this preoccupation with order was detrimental to the child's self-concept; it caused her to assume responsibilities beyond her proper sphere, to stress her purely imaginary failings, and so blame herself for happenings that were beyond her control.

It was of the utmost importance for the child to have an opportunity to establish consistent contact with a male adult who could aid her to recapture her faith that she could rely on such a person and have a relaxed and more predictable relationship with him. Also, since her detrimental behavior mechanisms were based on a strong anxiety feeling, it is apparent that this anxiety could only be effectively

---

[1] For similar ritualistic patterns emerging in times of anxiety, see Jean Piaget, *The Child's Conception of the World* (London, Routledge & Kegan Paul, 1951), Chapter IV, p. 156.

lessened by long and reassuring acquaintance with a person representative of the central object of her conflicts, i.e. her father. The observable improvements in Harriet's behavior patterns were no doubt attributable in no small measure to the fact that the nursery school provided her with this consistent presence of a male figure.

TOPICS FOR DISCUSSION

Chapter 7 *Harriet*

1. How may a "quest for the past" be reflected in a child's play?
2. How might a child who feels the need to be extremely orderly in her behavior be helped to express herself more freely?
3. How should the parent with whom the child remains cope with the child's questions concerning the absent parent?
4. What effects might the emotional climate of a home prior to its being becoming a broken one have upon the reaction of the child to the new situation?

Case 6
Philip:
A House Divided

BACKGROUND: *Philip; age 5.0 at entrance; mother 30, not work-*
ing at present; father 34, engineer; parents of the
child recently divorced; the child is in the custody
of the mother; no other children; taken care of
by mother or grandmother; spends alternate
week-ends with the father; normal birth, breast-
fed; high intelligence; good health.

Philip was brought into the group by his mother. He arrived
a few days later than the rest of the children since he had
recently moved to a new home with his mother. The child
seemed very bewildered, spoke to no one, shrugged his
shoulders and retreated when asked anything by the other
children. He seemed generally frightened and clung to his
mother. I suggested to her that Philip's visits to school be
limited to half a day for a while, and that she remain during
this time near the vicinity of the room. The child had recently undergone much emotional strain, and in being

placed in a nursery school, was now being asked to make
an additional, difficult adjustment. The mother complied
with my suggestions. Philip remained near the book shelves
the entire time of his first stay, aimlessly leafing through the
pages of books or looking out of the window. He showed no
interest in any of the other activities, nor did he speak to
any of the children. He carried with him a small cloth bag
filled with pebbles, which he emptied into his hand and
proceeded to count and recount an endless number of times.
He would not let any child come near the bag and hid it
quickly in his pocket when it seemed to arouse their
curiosity.

Philip spent the next few days in a similar manner. He
tended always to remain on the periphery of the group;
and at those times when the children were engaged in occupations in which they seemed particularly active and happy,
he was inclined, I soon noted, to be more than ever dejected, to the point of crying silently or hiding himself
behind a screen. Efforts on our part to encourage him to
join or to be an active onlooker, or simply to comfort him,
were met with further retreat and such statements as "You
can't help me," or "I don't care about their games." When
children asked him at these times to play with them or
questioned him as to why he was hiding, he would say, "I
don't know," and become very confused. They soon made
fewer efforts to include him in their games, thus isolating
him further.

During the following weeks, Philip slowly began to respond to the continuous efforts of my assistant and me to
make contact with him. But he would speak to me only
if the other children were some distance away and he could
be certain of my complete and undivided attention. His

conversation dealt often with abstract topics, topics that served to disguise his feelings about personal matters as well as about him immediate environment. He discussed with me at great length, for instance, how one could "build bridges from one house to another, so that people wouldn't have to go down in the streets all the time. That way, there wouldn't be so many people in the street all the time. And you could go places and nobody would even know about it." When I asked, "What kind of places?" he grew reticent at once: "I don't know. Secret places." During another conversation, he suggested that it would be good to have, "one of those machines that put your voice on a piece of tape. Then, anytime you wanted to hear somebody talk, you could just turn the machine on. And you wouldn't have to see them, but you could hear them talk."

If by chance, we were interrupted in our conversation by another child, or if, as often happened, the group demanded my attention, Philip's whole demeanor changed. Interest and animation gave way to dejection and retreat, sometimes to passive hostility. He would glare at the child in question, or at me; and he once flared up angrily, "I wanted to tell you something important. But now you spoiled it!"

One afternoon, when Philip's mother, after having remained near the classroom and constantly available to him for several weeks, asked the child: "Do you think you can stay by yourself now? You remember, I told you that I have to go and see about my job today." Upset and angry, Philip shouted at her: "Yes! Yes! Go ahead! Nobody has to wait for me. You can't help me here anyway." Taken aback, his mother tried to calm him: "I'll come back as soon as I can."

But Philip had turned away and gone to sit by himself in a corner of the room.

That afternoon, he began to sew pieces of felt together with cotton thread. Every few minutes he would cut the thread, rip out the stitches he had made, and start all over again. He continued to do this for the rest of the day and could not be deterred by any other activities. It was the first occupation he had attempted beyond looking at books or staring out of the window. During the following days, he occupied himself almost exclusively with sewing small bags of felt, which he then filled with beans or pebbles, and later embroidered. When he could not busy himself in this manner, he would return to books, sit inactively observing the actions of the other children, or if we played outdoors, walk on the cracks of the sidewalk in a repetitive fashion.

On calling for him one afternoon, Philip's mother saw the sewing he had been doing. She admired it, but somewhat embarrassedly hastened to explain that she had taught the child to sew about a year before, when he was ill. He had not done any sewing since, and she was surprised that he should show himself still interested in it. Another time, she remarked that Philip had grown up mostly among adults and had had very little opportunity to play with children. He spent a great deal of time with books or phonograph records of children's stories.

Philip showed in his behavior the great strain to which he had been subjected by the dissolution of his family. Its effects are seen in his general uncertainty and in his withdrawal from all new experiences which demanded from him an effort of adjustment. The tendency to remove himself from the scene of action was evident in his refusal to talk to the children or participate in their games and in his even more active retreat when asked to join the entire group. His anguish at making this retreat was expressed by his hiding and by his crying or otherwise giving way to sadness and discouragement.

Since new experiences were upsetting him, he relied on those activities which were familiar to him. They apparently formed the only safe base for his behavior and were comforting in that they did not demand a new adjustment. This reliance upon the past was variously indicated by his behavior: his continuous play with the cloth bag filled with pebbles which he had brought with him; going back to sewing, a long-discarded activity of his earlier childhood; his conversations with adults, with whom he had had past contacts, rather than children. In addition, Philip's general insecurity was reflected in his strong reaction against sharing the complete attention of an adult.

Philip's stories show a preoccupation with indirect wish-fulfilment. The actual wish is clothed in invention and fantasy; the desire to communicate with others is disguised. Bridges built between the houses made it possible to visit places without having to face the many people in the streets and without their knowledge. When asked directly, "What kind of places?" Philip immediately withdraws: "I don't know. Secret places." The houses one visits contain people (or a certain person) and by using bridges, one might be able secretly to see a person otherwise forbidden or inaccessible. In his second story, actually a variation on the first, we see again the indirect, mechanical device used to achieve contact with a person without the possible dangers involved in actually having to see him: "And you wouldn't have to see them, but you could hear them talk." Whether this desire to communicate with someone applied directly to the child's absent father could not at the moment be determined. But it is to be noted that in each instance it is the child who is in control of achieving this contact, whereas in real life, Philip exhibited great difficulty in even indirect contact with others. Actually, Philip did not converse with me. He simply made me an audience to a story he wished to tell.

At about this time, since I felt that Philip needed to make contact with children of his age, I placed his cot at rest-hour close to one of the most sociable and considerate of the boys. At first, Philip attempted to ward off any efforts of this boy to show friendliness. I tried to provide them with further opportunities to become acquainted with each other by placing them side by side at the lunch table and by asking them to share a book that Philip particularly liked. Philip, who was able to read a little, began to tell the other boy the story and explained some of the words beneath the pictures to him. The other boy was able to inspire interest in Philip for some other forms of play. As long as they were together, Philip seemed more content than usual. When, however, other children attempted to join their game, Philip withdrew immediately.

One day, Philip was watching his friend Bill building a railroad track out of blocks. Bill said, "This is going to be a big railroad track. It's going all the way to the other side of the world." "That's awfully far away," Philip commented. "So far you couldn't see this side at all. Not even from the highest building." "Well, the trains go as fast as a bullet," Bill said, "and that's fast. You can be there and back in a bang." Philip got very excited at this idea. He said animatedly, "That's a good one. All you have to do is pull the trigger. And you can go and see anybody you like."

Philip thought for a moment, then added, "I bet you could get to Queens so fast that nobody would even see you." (Philip's father lived in Queens.)

Philip continued to be interested in his former activities such as reading and sewing; he began, however, to branch out into painting and clay work. In his paintings, he chose the smallest brushes to work with and concentrated on very detailed work and limited areas located usually in the corners of the large sheet of paper. One girl, who was painting next to him, asked him once, "Aren't you going to put anything in the middle?" Philip answered, "No. It's too empty there." Another time, while he was at the easel, he painted two houses, one at each end of the paper. Then he asked me for cotton, and, dipping it in white paint, he proceeded to paste small dots of cotton over the surface separating the houses. When one of the children said to him, "Oh, it's snowing in your picture," he answered, "Yes, and the snow is so thick, you can't see anything when you look out the window."

I began to notice that sometimes at the very beginning of the week, Philip would be quite upset. He would refuse to participate in those activities which he had recently undertaken and would return to sitting apart from the other children, and to leafing aimlessly through the pages of books; or to occupying himself for long periods of time cutting up bits of paper. When Bill approached him at these times, he withdrew and would not answer his inquiries. Once, however, when Bill asked him, "Did something wrong happen?" Philip silently nodded his head. Bill continued, "What? You don't feel so good?" Philip answered, "I don't know. I never know where I'm supposed to feel good." Bill seemed puzzled and asked, "What do you mean?" But

Philip would not answer him. I later found out from the social worker's report that the child spent alternate weekends at his father's house in Queens. The strain of seeing his father, and then being once more removed from him undoubtedly accounted for this periodic behavior.

I also had a conference with Philip's mother in which she mentioned that the child was very upset after each stay with the father and that she worried, since it seemed to her that Philip brooded "just like his father," and seemed, "to get more harm than good out of seeing him." She seemed bitter about the divorce and said that if her husband had spent a little more time at home, "things wouldn't be where they are now." I suggested that it was important for Philip to have an outlet for his feelings through making friends with a child of his own age with whom he could share constructive experiences. I mentioned that perhaps she might invite Bill to come to Philip's house for a visit.

Through the formation of a friendship with Bill, Philip was enabled to better externalize some of his feelings and encouraged to extend his scope of personal and external experience. He was no longer limiting his attention to adults. This new relationship brought with it a widening of the scope of Philip's activities to include painting and clay work and the ability to communicate in the form of games rather than merely through abstract discussions.

In the incident of the railroad track, Philip at first expressed anxiety that "the other side of the world" is "awfully far away." But this was quickly followed by his subsequent excitement over the bullet-like trains conjured up by Bill and his delight that in these trains "All you have to do is pull the trigger. And you can go and see anybody you like." He then indicated whom he would like to go and see in this manner: "I bet you could get to Queens so fast that nobody could even see you." His adding that "nobody could even see" him reveals his feeling that, although he is drawn to his father, he wishes this fact not to be directly known.

This situation is further reflected in the earlier stories in which he went to visit "secret places" by the use of bridges so that he need not resort to the streets filled with people, and in his wish for a tape-recorder to hear the voice he desired to hear without having to risk the actual presence of the person. This need for secrecy and veiled reference probably had its roots in the obvious bitterness of the mother towards the father. Her attitude made it necessary for the child to refrain from directly referring to his desire to have the father near him, and also to disguise, even from himself, his need for such contact. We might also assume that the separation from the father was a painful emotional experience, and the fantasy which cloaks meetings with him or plans of reaching him serves as a device to lessen the severity of that painful experience by removing it from the world of actuality.

Further aspects of Philip's personality reveal themselves in his paintings. We see in the first merely a hesitation to proceed boldly into the large space and his tendency to remain involved in small details, paralleling his actions within the group. The fear of emptiness in the center of the page reflects the emptiness he feels in his own life because his family has become incomplete. In his explanation of the second painting, Philip expresses the confusion he feels by noting that there are two houses, separated by a cold, thick wall of snow, and that this barrier obscures vision. This confusion is shown even more clearly and directly in his conversation with Bill during a period when he is quite upset after a visit to his father: "I never know when I'm supposed to feel good."

Philip is quite exact in the interpretation of his dilemma. He has two homes and the vision between them is obscured. He does not feel good at either home since each one is incomplete, and he is, moreover, torn between loyalty for both of his parents and the reality of their separation. His mother's attitude towards the father is also a hindrance to Philip's arriving at an acceptance of his own position. Since, too, the mother resents those aspects of the father's personality which she sees reflected in the child and shows her resentment whenever similarities between the child and its father are evident, Philip, who is in great need of his mother's understanding, is forced to suppress the direct expression of his needs and to modify his behavior to please her or comply with her demands.

He resorts to fantasy and indirect expression to cope with the tremendous yearnings and emotional conflicts he is experiencing. But Philip shows how overpowering is the burden that has been put upon him by depression, by silent crying, and by resorting to such "magical" practices as counting the stones in his cloth bag, stepping repetitiously on cracks in the pavement, cutting papers aimlessly for long periods of time, and alternately sewing and ripping out what he has sewn. These activities can be interpreted as attempts to gain some small measure of control over his chaotic world.

Philip's contacts with me gave him an opportunity to express some of the feelings which he was not permitted to show for his father. Also, his relationship with me did not involve the hostility of his mother, as did his relationship with his father.

I proceeded during the course of the school year to work a great deal with Philip on an individual basis. It was necessary first of all to gain his trust and confidence by convincing him that I would be constantly available. It was important, too, that my behavior toward him be always consistent, since he needed above all a predictable and dependable relationship. As the realization that I would always help and reassure him became stronger, Philip became better able to accept interruptions in his conversations with me and gave evidence of feeling less resentment toward other children who received my attention.

Whereas formerly he had not participated in the more "masculine" activities such as woodwork and ball-playing, he now began to include these in his scope of interests. He did very exact work in the woodshop, starting at first with the construction of a simple wooden spool on which to wind the cotton thread he used for his sewing, but proceeding to making other more complex and masculine objects. He took great pride in his work, at one time remarking, "This is real man's work, isn't it?"

Philip's progress in the group proceeded slowly but noticeably. Formerly, when the children engaged in musical interpretation of stories, an activity which often took the form of very free pantomime and dance, he had hidden in the farthest corner of the room, preferably behind a screen, and had often wept. By degrees, the weeping stopped and he no longer hid, though he still remained far from the other children, observing them. He moved progressively closer as each week passed, until finally, at the end of the school year, he had gone so far as to take off his shoes as the other children did and sit in the circle with the rest of the group, although he still did not actively participate. He began, timidly at first, to respond to some of the advances made by other children. He had made a real friend in Bill and been able to enter into many new areas of experience. Philip's progress within the comparatively short space of a school year was indeed encouraging.

Summary:

In the case of Philip, we see in stark relief the ill effects on a child when both parents become objects of conflict, not only because of their separation but also because of their critical attitudes toward one another. The emotional conflict thus aroused in the child forced him to resort to fantasy in order to express his needs and desires. Uncertain of his own position he retreated from new experiences, preferring to rely upon familiar patterns of behavior and hoping thus to recapture the past and avoid facing the present. His use of magical practices, to the exclusion of more constructive activities, constituted a futile effort to gain some control over a world upon which he no longer felt able to depend.

Philip's ability to interpret his conflict, at first abstractly and then more directly, was a significant and positive sign. It showed a desire to communicate with others, no matter how much he felt he had to disguise this communication; and it provided him with some release from his tensions. It also made it possible for him ultimately to form a sustained relationship with another child, and with me, and so to proceed slowly to a better acceptance of reality.

Philip's behavior reflects to a more advanced degree those detrimental effects of infrequent presence of the father observed in the cases of children from normal homes: a general and pronounced confusion about his own standing within the family, about the respective functions of his parents, and about his own role as a boy. His behavior was such that nearly all new experience was excluded. He was in constant retreat from the demands of a world that needed to be explored. Only by very slow degrees and through painstaking efforts was progress toward widening Philip's scope of experience achieved.

The presence of a male adult in the school was in this case of the utmost importance, for it permitted the child consistent male contact without the conflicts and tensions that attended his contacts with his father.

Topics for Discussion

Chapter 8 *Philip*
1. What role might a teacher play in helping a young child through a crisis period such as a divorce or legal separation?
2. What factors should be considered before one attempts to evaluate how a child whose home has been broken should be helped?

Case 7

Tom:

Desertion by Death

BACKGROUND: *Tom: 5.0 years at entrance; mother 28, working; father died accidental death about a year previous; child sometimes taken care of by an aunt; 6 months' previous nursery school experience; only child; average intelligence; normal birth, bottle-fed, good health.*

Tom was brought into the group by his mother and was soon engaged in conversation with a few children whom he had known during his last semester in school. When his mother prepared to leave and told him that his aunt would be waiting for him at the school exit in the afternoon, he demanded, "Where are you going? To work?" His mother answered, "Yes, and I'm late now." As I was accompanying her to the door, the child came over again and said angrily, "What are you telling my mother?" When I told him that we were just saying good-bye, his mother added, "Yes. And aren't you going to say good-bye to me too?" Tom answered: "No. You'd better go to work. It's late."

During the following weeks, I noticed in Tom a general restlessness and an inability to concentrate for even a short time on any one activity. He began many things, but invariably soon became impatient and moved to another activity which he would begin with an enthusiasm that would quickly die. He participated in all areas of play, but never remained long enough to gain any real satisfaction from it. In his personal relationships, similarly, he moved from one group to another, mingling freely but erratically.

He often lost interest in the middle of a conversation. In the woodshop, he began a boat, a train, a birdhouse, all during the first week of school. Each time he started with great force and eagerness, but the moment the slightest difficulty arose in the work, he lost interest in the project, even though he was offered help or suggestions to enable him to finish it. On one occasion he began to build a dam in the sandpit with several other children, constructing various canals, rivers and bridges. He had suggested the entire activity to the children, but before he could enjoy the results of his labors, he suddenly noticed another group of children playing with a jump-rope, called, "I'll be back later," and ran off. He jumped twice over the rope then wandered away to still another group, and never did return to the sandpit.

The one activity which did hold his interest for longer periods was playing on the swings. He took great joy in being pushed by another child or by one of the teachers. He usually sang softly to himself at these times or repeated a few words over and over again, using a phrase whose meaning remained unclear to me for some time: "One . . . two . . . three, Tommy went up the tree"; it was sometimes varied with: "One . . . two . . . three, who's that sitting on my knee?"

Rest hour was always very difficult for Tom. He tossed a great deal, played with the cot, and when given a toy or a book to calm him, managed to remain quiet for only a few minutes before losing interest in the object and beginning to fidget again. He ate little and often neglected the food on his plate.

When he sat at the table of the woman teacher, he seemed to be concerned chiefly with obtaining her attention and blocking all questions of other children directed towards her. This kind of behavior was noticeable also in the other school activities when he was in her vicinity. He followed her closely, with an insistent, "Can I ask you something?" Once he had obtained her attention, he would jealously guard his conversation, not allowing any other child to participate. If they did enter the conversation he would attempt to shut out their remarks by talking in an excessively loud voice, or he would take over their questions and present them as though they were his own. Sometimes his need to obtain her attention was so great, that after insisting upon having it, he would become confused and say: "I forget what I wanted to tell you. Can I stay here until I remember?"

On the other hand, he was very critical of her. He noted very carefully what clothes she wore, commented on changes in her appearance, and often expressed his dislike of certain garments. This fault-finding occurred most frequently when she was absorbed in working with other children and became most violent whenever she was involved in a conversation with me and could not immediately comply with his demand for attention. On those occasions, he would mock her, saying, for example, "You have an ugly dress today," or "I don't like your funny-colored shoes," and would walk angrily away from her. Later in the day, however, he would usually privately assure her that her dress was "gorgeous," or that he liked "the shiny spots" in her hair.

Towards me, Tom's behavior was quite different. He watched me a great deal during the first few days, though hardly ever speaking to me or attempting to attract my attention. If I approached him, he always seemed tense and made some excuse to get away: "I have to hurry now; They're waiting for me over there," or "I didn't finish building my block house and somebody can trip if I don't straighten it up."

Whenever I read or told stories to the children, Tom was extremely restless and could not seem to concentrate or remember the events I had recounted. He often asked a neighbor, "What did he say happened before?" but never attempted to ask me personally. I noted a decided difference in his response when the woman teacher told stories. Although he showed some of the same difficulty in concentrating and remembering, he would ask her, at the risk of interrupting the entire sequence of events in the story, to repeat what she had said and would refuse explanations offered by another child.

Tom showed definite signs of hostility towards me. If I were in charge of the rest period, he refused to use the blanket I gave him; and, on one occasion, he threw the toy I offered him under the bed, saying, "If you don't watch out, I'm going to put you under the bed too," and began to laugh nervously. Another time, his plans for me were even more drastic. A number of children were building a "space ship" out of cardboard boxes and pieces of wood.

Tom happened to be in the vicinity and asked one of them, "What's it going to be?" They all answered excitedly, "A space rocket!" or, "A Mars Clipper!" Tom repeated: "A Mars Clipper! That's fine. We can put Everett in it and send him away." One of the children answered: "But it's not big enough for all of us. He'll take up too much room." To this Tom replied excitedly: "No, not all of us. Just him, all alone. We'll shoot him off to Mars and leave him there." As he was saying this, he looked in my direction and raised his voice so that I could be sure of hearing what my fate was to be.

Tom mingled well with the children, was well liked in the group, and had many friends. He never started a dispute, but was often the arbitrator in arguments, separating the two opponents or taking the side of the child whom he felt to be in the right if he thought he was not capable of defending his position. Sometimes the children called upon him, rather than on the adults present, to help them settle a dispute, which he did with great seriousness and utmost justice.

He was especially concerned, if the injustice concerned a girl and the offender was a boy. On one such occasion, a girl in the group had brought some oak leaves to school and had given each child two leaves to use as he wished. One of the boys, however, decided that he wanted more than his allotted share, and when the girl refused to give him any more, saying that she had given the same number to each of the children, he tore the leaves out of her hand and started to run away. Tom immediately went after him, saying "You better give those leaves back to her." The boy answered: "They're not your leaves. You can't tell me what to do." Tom retorted: "Those are hers. And you're a sissy if you take them." This statement seemed to take effect, for the boy gave back the leaves.

Once Tom brought some shoe polish to school and began shining the shoes of some of the children. He had arranged a few chairs for his "customers" to sit on, and was calling, "A dime a shine!" getting payment for his work in bits of silver paper. One of the girls, whose shoes he had nearly finished shining, was told by the boy in line behind her: "Come on. Hurry up and get off that chair. I have to have a shine too." When she didn't answer, he tried to push her off the chair. Tom got up from his kneeling position, put down his brush and with a scowl said, "Anybody who pushes doesn't get a shine."

As we have noted, Tom's behavior revealed general restlessness and inability to concentrate long enough on an activity to be able to enjoy it. There was a constant shifting of interest even in his personal relations, making for erratic and temporary involvements. He showed a particular desire to have the attention of the woman teacher, using ruses, flattery contrasted with mockery, and direct bids for attention, sometimes at the expense of other children. (It is interesting to note that in his behavior with other children, however, Tom insisted on absolute justice and would not allow one child to obtain something at the expense of another.) His demands upon her became most excessive when he felt that his position with her was threatened by the demands of the other children, and even more strikingly, when he thought he was competing with an adult male for her interest. His attacks upon her when she was conversing with me and could not give him her immediate attention paralleled his outburst of hostility when I was speaking to his mother on the first day of school.

At the beginning of the school year, Tom showed tension in my presence and a desire to be out of my immediate vicinity; but he seemed to feel that he could not directly remove himself without offering some rational excuse for his actions. Somewhat later, he began to be less concerned with hiding his feelings and became definitely hostile to me. He apparently wanted to make sure I knew how he felt about me, raising his voice, for example, to make certain I had heard his plans to "send me to Mars." He was, of course, not merely testing my reactions to his hostility; he was also trying to attract my attention by his remarks. Tom clearly did not wish to be dependent on me. He did not ask me to repeat parts of the story which he had been unable to remember, and refused emphatically the blanket which I offered him during the rest hour. He freely accepted these services from the woman teacher, however.

Tom's attacks upon me were childlike and his threats fantastic. On the other hand, his attacks on the woman teacher or on his mother took the more adult form of realistic criticism. Then, too, these attacks took place when the child felt that his position with them was threatened, whereas in my case they were intended to keep me at a distance.

The two conferences which I had with Tom's mother during the first part of the school year revealed little about the child's home life or about her attitude toward her son or her deceased husband. Her remarks were general and she seemed preoccupied mainly with her work and responsibilities. She did say to me, however, that it was difficult for her to cope with all of her child's demands and that since the death of her husband she had had to be "father and mother to Tom," which, of course, "was a great deal to ask."

Because these interviews were generally unproductive I consulted the social worker's reports for further insight into the home life of the child. I learned that Tom's mother had considered remarrying, but that Tom had reacted violently against the man in question and that she had therefore abandoned the idea temporarily. I learned further that ever since the sudden accidental death of Tom's father, Tom had shown an extreme attachment to his mother, not wanting to let her out of his sight for months after the accident. He had also found it extremely difficult to allow her to leave him even for a few hours at the beginning of his attendance at nursery school.

One day, a few of the children were telling a collective story, each participating in the development of the plot. One girl began the story by telling of three tug-boats pulling a big barge of coal. One tug-boat was called "Charley," and he was the biggest and strongest of the three; the next was "Bella," a lady tug-boat, with all kinds of flags and ribbons; last came "Baby-Tug-boat," who was huffing and puffing and had the highest whistle on the river. In fact, he whistled so much that all the people who saw the little tug-boat, laughed. At this point, the girl stopped and Tom said that he wanted to continue.

His portion of the story went as follows: "One day there was a big storm. And they all had to work hard, because the waves were this high (Tom stood up and held his hand above his head to indicate their height). All of a sudden the big tug-boat was gone. They didn't know where. They looked for him all over the river. The little tug-boat whistled so high, he should have heard it. But he didn't come back. So, they had to work all alone." After Tom had told his part of the story, he wouldn't wait to hear what the next child had to add but got up and left the area, visibly agitated.

Tom's story provides us with a new insight into his behavior. We see that the big tug-boat named "Charley" suddenly disappears, just as Tom's father suddenly was gone from the scene. The anguish provoked by this event is reflected in the story by the search all over the river and the frantic whistling of the smallest tug-boat. This anguish, however, is mingled with a feeling of reproach: "He should have heard the whistle. But he didn't come back." It would seem, then, that Tom felt his father had the power to come back if only he wanted to. The family thus abandoned by the father is unfairly burdened because of his absence, and there is a mingling of sadness and resentment in the statement: "So they had to work all alone."

We can see that these conceptions of the child are reflected in his behavior toward the woman teacher, his mother, and myself. His desire not to share the attention of the teacher with anyone was, of course, closely correlated with his reactions toward his mother. His unwillingness to form a close relationship with me and his show of resentment on various occasions indicated that he had transferred to me some of the resentment he harbored at being "abandoned" by his father. In addition, his attitude probably also indicated a fear of being hurt again. If he were to allow an adult male to be close to him, he would be running the risk of being "abandoned" again.

The emotional upheaval wrought in his mother when Tom's father died probably led the child to feel that since this disappearance was the cause of her unhappiness, his father had done her an injustice and that the injustice extended, also, to himself. Tom yearned for his father and desired to have him return, but, on the other hand, he felt resentment towards him for causing pain to his mother and himself by not returning. Tom's extreme concern with preventing boys from being unjust to girls was, of course, a by-product of this resentment. Tom's threats and angry remarks to me were intended, as we have noted, to test my responses and to attract my attention.

In the latter part of the school year, the other side of his feelings toward his father, his yearning and need for him, began to manifest itself in his behavior toward me. One day, quite suddenly, he came over to me and said, "Can I ask you something?" When I said yes, he went on, "Can you pick me up, so I can get the puzzle on the top shelf up there?" Actually, there was a small stepladder provided for this purpose, which Tom himself had often used. When I had picked him up, he seemed to forget about the puzzle and asked me whether I would give him a horseback ride. I promised to do so as soon as we got to the outdoor playground, and he was careful to remind me of this promise when we arrived there later in the day.

At about this time also he began to give me drawings he had made, saying: "I want you to keep this. And remember I gave it to you." He would ask me days later whether I still had the drawings and on several occasions even asked me to produce them again to make certain that this was really so. He began to show less tension when I spoke to the woman teacher and he had to wait for a moment until she could give him her attention, or if I addressed a few words to his mother when she came to call for him. Once I took his hand as we were crossing a street on one of our excursion trips. When we had reached the opposite side-

walk and I released it, he said to me somewhat reproach-
fully, "Why did you let go of my hand?" And when I said,
"I thought you'd like to walk on ahead with the other
children, " he answered: "No, I want to stay with you. Hold
my hand." In general, he now seemed to wish to be near
me and became, in fact, rather demonstrative towards me.

One incident which occurred at this time revealed most
poignantly how much in need the child was of this close relationship with an adult male. At the beginning of the
school year, it will be remembered, while rocking himself
on the swings, Tom had repeatedly uttered the phrases,
"One . . . two . . . three . . . , Tommy went up the tree," and
"One . . . two . . . three . . . , who's that sitting on my knee?"
One day, during the latter part of the school year, while I
was pushing him on the swings, Tom again uttered the first
of these phrases. When I commented, "That's a good
rhyme," he volunteered, "Yes, my daddy taught me that."
The next day, while I was telling a story to the children, he
came over and asked me quietly, "Can I come and sit on
your knees?" He remained there until I had finished the
story.

Summary:

In Tom's case, we see clearly enough how the emotional
upheaval caused by the death of a father may be reflected
in the behavior of the child. Tom gave evidence of general
restlessness and an inability to relate consistently to any
person or to stick to an activity, behavior indicative of his
upset emotions and general uncertainty. More specifically,
his understanding of death being incomplete, the father's
disappearance is mystifying to the child and he tends to

interpret it as an act of injustice. Consequently he tended to mistrust men, as seen in his behavior toward me and toward the man who was considering marrying his mother.

Tom's behavior toward women gave evidence that his mother and other adult females now received the affection formerly shared by his two parents. Tom's tension when the attention of his mother or his female teacher was not centered exclusively upon him reflected his fear of losing the sole providers of his needs that remained to him.

His relationships with children reflected the concept he had developed of his own role. Because he is a member of the male sex and because his father's death had resulted in his seeing men as perpetrators of injustice, he felt compelled toward some form of compensatory behavior. He became the guardian of justice, especially when it was a question of seeing that justice was done to girls. He, in other words, had taken it upon himself to right the injustice he considered men capable of. In like manner he assigned to himself the role of protecting his mother from the injustice which he believed she might again be subjected to through close relationship with a man.

We see, then, that the sudden removal of Tom's father from the family structure seriously distorted the child's view of himself and of the world about him and that this distortion was reflected in many aspects of his behavior. The nursery school provided Tom with the opportunity to form a new and stable relationship with an adult male. This relationship enabled him to externalize the positive feelings he still harbored toward his father and to begin, at least, to correct the distorted image of the male that was in turn distorting his view of the world and of himself.

TOPICS FOR DISCUSSION

Chapter 9 *Tom*

1. What factors should be considered before one attempts to help a child who is suddenly confronted with a death in the family?
2. Should reference to the death of a parent always be avoided in discussion with the offspring of the deceased?
3. What might be good avenues of approach to the problem of inculcating in a child a realistic view of death?
4. Do you think it is a good idea to discuss the idea of death with children, even when there is no specific need to do so?

Case 8

Judy:

The Phantom Father

BACKGROUND: *Judy: age 4.7 years at entrance; mother 30, works at home as dressmaker; father died when Judy was 2 months old; one sister, age 7; no previous nursery school experience; average intelligence; normal birth, breast-fed for first 1½ months, then bottle-fed; physical examination shows the child to be in good health, but frail and underweight.*

When Judy entered the group, she was hesitant in her new surroundings and clung to her mother, meanwhile watching the children and the general proceedings. After a while, she became interested in a doll-carriage, chose a toy bear to put into it, and began to wheel it back and forth in a corner of the room. When her mother saw that Judy was busy and seemed content with her occupation, she said to her: "I'll be out in the hall. If you need me, you can find me there." Judy answered, "All right, I'll call you if the baby cries." Then she patted the bear and sat down with the carriage in a quiet corner.

During the first few days, Judy played mostly alone. Later, she began to bring some of her own toys and belongings to school, a toy elephant, an embroidered handkerchief, a toy-watch. She used these objects to start conversations with the children. Their attention permitted her to become briefly the center of attraction. Without their aid, however, she seemed to feel awkward with the other children, at a loss for words, and unsure of how to join a group.

When the objects she brought to school no longer aroused and held the interest of the children, she resorted to a new device. She began to tell elaborate stories about the toys she had at home. For example, she told one of the children to whom she had previously shown her toy elephant, "I went to the circus last night and you know what I saw?" The other child said eagerly, "You tell me." Judy continued, "I saw elephants as big as my shoe. So I took one home and put him next to my bed." The other girl asked in a surprised tone: "Next to your bed? Why did you put him next to there?" Judy answered very seriously, "Don't you know? So he can wake me up in the morning. He blows a funny noise from his nose." The other child laughingly interrupted, "For real?" and Judy answered, "Of course. Only he doesn't always wake me up. Sometimes he forgets and he sleeps all day."

At other times, she produced these stories when the children were engaged in a new activity and she was uncertain about her ability to participate. For example, one day while some of the children were dressing up in the dramatic play area to go on a "picnic," Judy just stood and watched. The preparations for the picnic consisted of packing food, dressing for the various roles, and cleaning the "cars" for the occasion. One of the children called to Judy, "Aren't you coming? What are you going to be?" Judy answered hesitatingly, "I don't know." The child called again, "Come on, anyway. It's fun. And there's lots of room in the car." Judy seemed to think the proposal over, then said, "I don't need a car. I can come flying after you on my magic handkerchief." She pulled a crumpled handkerchief from the pocket of her dress, adding: "Here it is. I just got back from a trip. That's why it's all wrinkled." The other child said, "Let me try it." Judy shook her head: "It won't do you any good. It only flies for me. You've got a car to ride in anyway," and she pointed to the wooden bench which one of the boys was shining with a piece of cloth.

At first, this method of Judy's to participate at least indirectly in group activities was successful. But although her fantastic stories were momentarily interesting, the children soon learned that Judy herself did not make a very satisfactory play companion. She too often tended to participate only indirectly in their games and activities and to avoid realistic contact with them. Her stories almost always found an audience because of Judy's appealing imagination; but as soon as the children found an activity which was more absorbing, she was left alone. She would then rely on play of an isolated sort, such as weaving, painting, and sewing, but she remained constantly aware of the other children and on the look-out for some new opportunity to arouse their interest again.

Judy showed a general acceptance of the woman teacher that included a good deal of trust and some dependency, though her manner was somewhat reserved. She did not

show a reliance upon special devices or elaborate stories
to gain her attention. She had a tendency, however, to veil
her feelings somewhat and to resort to indirect methods of
expressing her needs. At one time, for example, when she
appeared at a loss how to join a game of ball in the playground and obviously wanted help from the teacher, she
said to her, "They don't have enough children to play that
game." When the teacher suggested, "Suppose you go and
ask them if you can play," Judy answered: "No, you; I
think my tooth will hurt when I talk."

Her approach with me was very different. When she first
entered the group, she watched me a great deal and seemed
to wish to remain near me. She showed great curiosity about
my actions and appearance, and was intrigued by the idea
of my taking care of children. Although I was totally unfamiliar to her, as soon as she arrived she turned to me
directly, questioned me, and did not veil her interest or
curiosity; she expressed her feelings openly, without resorting to any special mechanisms. Instead, she seemed completely absorbed in the process of exploring various aspects
of my personality and behavior.

On one of the first days of school, for example, she came
up to me and silently watched as I prepared some tools in
the woodshop. Then she touched my arm with her fingers
and said, "What a lot of hair! Why do you grow hair on
your arms?" I smiled and answered, "You have hair on
your arm too. Everybody does. Only yours is so fine, you
have to look much harder to see it." When she went on,
"My mother doesn't have such big hairs on her arms,"
I said, "Well, men usually have more hair on their arms
than women." She touched my arm again and seemed to

consider the matter seriously, then studied her own arm, holding it up to the light.

She also showed surprise at the fact that I took care of the children's needs. When I put the food on their plates at lunch time, she remarked, "This is fun. You look just like the man in the restaurant. All you need is a big white hat." When I sat down at the same table with the children to eat, she said, "Are you always going to sit here and eat with us, just like her?" and she pointed to the woman teacher. Another time, when the children had begun to rest in the afternoons and I remained in the room to read them a story, Judy inquired, "You're going to stay here and watch us rest?" The following day, she remarked to me, "You sure know how to fix blankets. Will you fix mine tomorrow, just the way you did for Fred?" (I had tucked the ends of the blanket around Fred's feet because he had complained of being cold).

Once, when I had brought shaving material to school for the children to play with and they had taken it to the dramatic-play corner where the mirror, soap, water and towels were to be found, Judy looked puzzled and asked, "What's that for?" One child answered, "That's to shave. We're going to shave just like the big men do." She turned to me then and asked, "Do you shave?" I nodded and she continued, "But what's it mean to shave?" One boy said, "That's when you cut your beard off so you don't scratch when you kiss." The others laughed. One girl remarked, "First, you got to put lots of soap on your chin. My daddy looks like a snowman in the morning." The boy added, "Here, I'll show you," and he proceeded to lather his face. Judy came up to me again and asked, "Do you do that too?" I answered, "Yes, I have to or my face gets too rough." She

carefully touched my chin and said: "It's not so rough . . .
Oh, yes it is, when you rub it like this." After this incident,
she asked me on several occasions whether she could touch
my face until she seemed to have fully satisfied her curiosity
in this matter.

As we have noted, in relationships with her peers, Judy
showed a lack of confidence in her ability to make direct
contact with them, on the basis of her personal standing
alone. She felt it necessary to resort to using objects or telling
stories of a fanciful nature in an attempt to interest them,
and, later, to cover up what seemed to be a fear of participating directly in games with them. This fear might have
been based on a feeling of inadequacy about entering into
an unfamiliar activity without the aid of a device which
she believed would raise her status in their eyes. When,
however, the objects she brought to school or the stories
she told did not succeed in holding the children's interest,
she found herself at a loss as to how to act and isolated herself from them. However, she was not at ease being on the
periphery of the group and was constantly on the alert for
other devices and new opportunities to recapture their interest and gain status in their eyes.

Even with the woman teacher, with whom she appeared
to feel generally at ease, she showed a tendency to avoid
direct reference to her needs and to employ veiled allusions.
A similar behavior pattern was noted on the first day of
school when Judy felt it necessary, even with her mother, to
use the "baby" she was wheeling in the doll carriage as a
spokesman for her own feelings, expressing thus very indirectly the need she probably felt for her mother's reassurance. When her mother told her that she would be in the
hall and that Judy could find her there if she needed her,

the child had answered, "I'll call you if the baby cries."

Toward me, however, Judy responded directly, with curiosity and actual exploration. In our relationship an obviously stronger need was at work and she abandoned the mechanical devices she felt compelled to use with others in favor of a straightforward exploration and a direct show of feelings. Her greatest concern seemed to be with finding out what my qualities, my role, and my functions were in relation to children. She wanted to gain information about me (and, of course, about men in general). Her lack of knowledge about males extended even to such elementary facts as shaving, the roughness of a man's beard, or the growth of hair on a man's arms. Her desire for information was coupled with a wish to be taken care of by me, once my role became clear to her and she realized that it included the care of the children in the group.

In a conference with Judy's mother, I learned that Judy was close to her older sister, who had for a long time been her principal playmate. The child's mother said she was having difficulty lately in coping with Judy's questions about her dead father. Her older child had previously gone through a similar period of curiosity about the subject. She mentioned that Judy had, of course, previously remarked on the fact that other children had fathers and she had none and had questioned her about it. However, now that she was being exposed to more children and to closer relationships with them and also to daily contact with me, she had become extremely preoccupied with this matter, wished to know all about her father, and had on one occasion remarked, "It's not fair. The other children all have one."

When I told Judy's mother that nursery school always

represents a transition period in which a child makes many new adjustments and that it was to be hoped that Judy would develop new conceptions which would aid her to see her family position in a more acceptable light, the mother responded by saying, "I hope so. In a way it's lucky that she has a man for a teacher. I never remarried, and it has been hard for her, always living in a house full of women."

About this time, Judy began to develop a new behavior pattern in her dealings with the other children. I noted now that her stories had changed in substance and had begun to deal mainly with an imaginary figure whom she called her father. The first time I noticed this was during a conversation in which various children told what plans they had for Christmas, what presents they wanted, and where they would go. One child had just finished saying, "I asked Santa Claus for a dump-truck. And my daddy said he was asking for a new hat." Another added, "We're going to the country." Judy, who had been listening quietly, suddenly said, "That's nothing. My daddy knows Santa Claus. And he's going to take me to see him." When another child asked, "Does he really?" Judy nodded and went on, "And that isn't all. My daddy can drive a sled and we're going way out to the country. And he's gonna have three new hats for Christmas."

Another day, once more apparently aroused by the conversation of the other children about members of their family, Judy again referred to her "father." The children were looking through story books and one of them happened to choose one which dealt with the various jobs that fathers have, illustrated with pictures of men in costumes appropriate to their occupation. One boy said, "That's where my father works," pointing to a man in an office. Another child leafed through the pages, then exclaimed, "Here he is! In the grocery store. Only my father doesn't have a mustache."

Judy came over and said: "Let me see that book. I bet they haven't got a picture of my daddy in there." A child asked, "What does he do?" Judy didn't answer but turned the pages swiftly until she had come to the end of the book. Then she said, "This book is no good. My daddy can do more than anybody in those pictures." One of the boys said laughingly, "Can he lift up this building?" Judy answered, "Sure. He could lift up this building anytime." Another boy said, "I bet you he couldn't lift up a mountain," and one girl added, "How about flying? Can he fly?" Judy answered excitedly, "Yes! yes! I told you he could do anything! He can go faster than—faster even than the birds!" The children listened fascinated, although not quite knowing what to make of these statements. But Judy seemed content with the effect of her story upon them.

Meanwhile, Judy had come to me quite a few times with questions such as whether I had any children at home, what I did every day after school, if it were hard to "tie that funny knot" in my tie, why men had so many pockets in their clothes, why I had "such a big bump" on my throat, all of which indicated a constant search for information about men. Obviously, she needed to gain insight into the nature and functions of men and to establish a realistic picture of them for herself. On the other hand, she had to conceal her lack of personal acquaintance with men and the painful fact that she did not possess a father by the use of stories which created an idealized father-figure, more powerful than the actual fathers of the other children.

We see reflected in the behavior of Judy an apparent con-

cern with the incompleteness she senses in her family structure as compared with that of the other children. This concern, first expressed to her mother, is later mirrored in her
stories dealing with an imaginary father. She thus com-
pensates for the lack she feels in not having a father and
for her sense of inadequacy when she compares herself to
other children. By making the imaginary father a more
powerful figure than the actual fathers of the other children, Judy is able to feel that she has somewhat equalized
her position with theirs. Since this mechanism of fantasy
construction can only partly satisfy her need, she is constantly driven to reconstruct, with variations, the same theme
in her stories in order to lessen the ever-renewed tension.
Her need here is to wipe out her feeling of inadequacy. She
shows little yearning for an actual father. Having had no
real experience of a father-child relationship, Judy has not
yet been fully able to visualize what she is missing by being
deprived of it. She interprets her deprivation almost solely
as a lowering of her status.

The fantastic nature of her stories, which at first awed
and fascinated the children, created new conflicts for Judy
when her creations became so exaggerated as time went
on that the children began to challenge their validity, sometimes refusing point-blank to believe them. For example, a
man was washing windows of a neighboring building one
day, supported by a series of hooks and belts. The children
were watching and commenting on his activities. Each
time the man unhooked his belt to switch it to the next
window and for an instant hung suspended by only one
side of his belt, the children exclaimed with great excitement, "Boy, look at him swing on one leg," or "I'd be scared,
all the way up there."

A short time later the children decided to reenact the man's work in the form of dramatic play. One boy had a sponge and stood on a stepladder, washing the blackboard on the wall. Judy handed him a bucket of water and gave him an old belt she had found to put around his waist. She said, "You better take this, so you don't fall." The boy answered, "That's right. I forgot. He had a belt to hold him up." Judy added, "You should see my daddy. He never needs a belt to hold him up. He could walk right up the side of a building, he's such a good climber." One of the children remarked: "You're kidding. Who ever heard of somebody walking up a house just like that." Another added, "Oh, you're always telling stories. You think your father can do anything." Judy answered in an agitated tone, "He can, I know he can!" But the first child remarked again, "It's just make-believe," and another boy added, "Why doesn't he come to school and show us, if he's so good." Judy burst into tears and ran away from the children.

Judy's stories about her imaginary father stopped abruptly after this incident; she became very much dejected, hardly played with other children, and began to be absent from school. When I spoke to her mother, she told me that the child didn't want to come to school. Judy said that the other children made fun of her, and she complained that she did not feel well. I then suggested to Judy's mother that it might be wise for me to telephone her home and speak to the child myself. When I did so, I attempted to reassure her that the children missed her and that we would all like to see her in school again. She said to me, "Do you want me to come to school? And do you want to see me?" When I said that I did, she remarked, "I think maybe I'll be better soon." At the end of our conversation, she added, "You wait for me. I think I'm coming tomorrow."

Upon her return, the children greeted her as usual and she seemed relieved when they made no reference to the incident which had upset her so much. From this time on, though, she spent less time playing with them and remained mostly in my vicinity. She showed a desire to have me give her a great deal of attention and to include her in most of the things I was doing. In turn, I often asked her to help me with my work of preparing materials, so that we functioned as a team on many occasions. This seemed to give her great pleasure. Sometimes in talking to me she referred to me as "daddy," and one time, catching herself in the middle of the word, said, "I started to call you daddy." She thought for a moment, then added, "Children like their daddies, don't they?" I answered "Yes," and said nothing further about her remark.

It became apparent at this time that an important transition had taken place within Judy. The rejection by the other children of her imaginary father had made her aware that she no longer depend upon this fantasy to compensate for her not having a father. There followed first an emotional outburst, then an abrupt abandonment of the use of fantasy, and finally a withdrawal from the scene of tension.

Upon her return to school after my telephone call, her behavior changed. Whereas she had formerly fabricated an imaginary father, she now proceeded to create an imaginary relationship with a real person—myself. This transition was a positive one since it brought the child closer to reality and might be directed into the development of a valuable relationship. I decided to put no undue emphasis on her use of the word "daddy" to refer to me and to treat it as I would any other name she might have applied to me. I wished to allow her freedom in the expression of her feelings and an opportunity to gain confidence in her relationship with me so that she might herself come to feel that she could like me and be liked in return, without having to see me in the light of an imaginary father.

Some time later, towards the end of the school year, Judy gave an indication that she was indeed moving closer to reality concerning her substitution of me for her father. One day she came over to me and said quite suddenly, "Do you know, I don't have a real daddy. I never saw him at all." I answered, "Yes, I know, Judy." She went on, "And when I call you daddy, I know you're not really. But it makes me feel good anyway." I then said, "It makes me feel good, too, because it means that you like me. But you know, you can call me Everett and I'll know you like me just the same." She seemed to accept this statement and added, "All right, sometimes I'll call you Everett and sometimes the other. And you'll know what I mean." After this, interestingly enough, she seemed to feel much less need to call me "daddy," and, in fact, she did so only on one other occasion.

During the remainder of the school year, her relationship with me continued to be close. She became better adjusted to the group and began to mingle more freely with the children without any apparent need for special devices to help her make contact with them.

Summary:

In the case of Judy, we have noted a series of steps in the development of her behavior pattern and her attitudes, each one an outgrowth and modification of the last, leading finally to a better general adjustment in the child. At the beginning of the school year, Judy showed signs of uncertainty and a feeling of inadequacy. The feeling of inadequacy was based mainly on the disadvantage she sensed in not having a father when she compared herself with other children. The effects of these feelings can be seen in her use of various mechanisms aimed at assuring her of acceptance by the children in the group. These mechanisms grew more complicated as her need to be accepted grew greater. Thus, objects were succeeded by rather fantastic stories, and these stories were finally focused upon an imaginary father, a completely unrealistic figure cloaked with powers far beyond those of the actual fathers of the other children.[1]

The highly unrealistic nature of the fantasy father was the result, first of all, of Judy's almost complete ignorance of men, as demonstrated by her many expressions of surprise at even the most elementary of men's attributes and physical make-up. Secondly, there was her great need to create a father who by his idealized and wonder-working nature could satisfy her desire for greater status. The child was simply attempting to satisfy a real need in an unreal way. Concomitantly the nature of the fantasy also indicated Judy's lack of real comprehension of a father-child relationship: she interpreted her deprivation of it as a lowering of status rather than a loss of a vital emotional tie. At no time did the fantasy-father show that the child can expect a father to provide love, close contact, protection, or fulfill the many other needs usually met by a real father.

Since Judy's main concern seemed to be the raising of her

---

[1] Orphans frequently show this tendency to speak of their dead father as if he were alive or could be brought back to life, or as if he were a god with miraculous properties. See D. Burlingham and A. Freud, *Enfants sans famille,* Presses Universitaires de France, Paris, 1949.

status to equality with that of the other children, she needed their approval and their acceptance of her fantasy. When her fantasy was abruptly challenged, she apparently realized the futility of her efforts. The entire fantasy structure collapsed and she was left with the realization that she could not escape into the realm of fantasy and expect to cope in this way with real situations. As a result, she was thrown into severe emotional upheaval and consequently removed herself entirely from the scene of conflict.

Upon her return to school, what had formerly been a compensatory device, became a bridge to a more basic approach to her problem. After the emotional crisis provoked by the challenge of the fantasy structure, Judy's behavior changed. Instead of indirect attempts to fulfil her needs, she now proceeded to draw upon a live image of the father, that is, myself. The nature of Judy's demands upon me became themselves more realistic too, by virtue of the comparative reality of this new image. In other words, this new image could actually supply male affection and understanding which until now had been completely lacking in her life and which she consequently could not comprehend. An imaginary relationship intended to supply needs which were in turn conceived on an unreal basis had now been replaced by a real human relationship with only a tinge of fantasy.

As noted above, I felt it important to maintain this assumed relationship for a while, and to allow her to call me her father. Had this relationship been discouraged, or had it, on the other hand, been reinforced by overt encouragement, it might have been repressed or become obsessive; then the possibility of turning it into more positive channels might have been destroyed. Instead, Judy was permitted a period of adjustment in which she herself could effect a transition between her former involvement with fantasy and her later ability to formulate her desire more realistically.

She had the opportunity, moreover, repeatedly to reinforce her newly-acquired concept of an actual male figure. She was finally able to realize that to profit from a relationship with me it was not necessary for her to clothe me in fantasy nor to consider me her "real" father; she came to understand that she could be close to me on more realistic terms. In addition, Judy had begun to realize more clearly what an emotional tie between father and child can mean: "I started to call you daddy. . . . Children like their daddies, don't they?"

No one can doubt that the environment of the nursery school itself and the positive influence of the other children were basic to the progressive improvement in Judy's attitudes and behavior. But it is equally true that the presence of an adult male was exceedingly important in this development. My presence furnished her, first, with an object for her search for information concerning the attributes and functions of men; secondly, a kind of substitute image that might meet some of her needs when the fantasy structure could not do so; then, a somewhat more realistic father figure to whom she could relate in a less fantastic fashion; and finally, an adult male with whom she could enter into a healthy, realistic relationship.

Throughout all this progression, Judy's basic need remained unchanged. But what had occurred by end of the school year was an important change in the child's comprehension of that need, in her expression of it, and in the object of her attempts to have it met. It is apparent that I could not be for Judy a true substitute for the father she so much desired, an outcome which would not have been desirable even if it could have been achieved. I could, however, fulfil the important function of becoming the representative of the male figure upon which she could formulate a better concept of a father and a more realistic picture of men in general.

TOPICS FOR DISCUSSION

Chapter 10 *Judy*

1. Do most young children have imaginary companions? When should a parent or teacher be concerned about this phenomenon?
2. Why do children have imaginary companions? What role do they play in the life of the child?
3. Is it important to consider the personality of the imaginary companion?

PART IV

OVERVIEWS AND RECOMMENDATIONS

The Missing Male:
Common Denominator
of Cases and Conflict

IN EACH of the first four cases the behavior and attitudes of the child showed the effects of insufficient contact with the father or other male adults. The child showed, if not a wrong orientation toward the male role, at least an insufficient acquaintance with it; he showed uncertainty or conflicting attitudes in regard to men. He was likely to have an incorrect or too limited concept of the functions and characteristics of men.

This distortion resulted in a concomitant misunderstanding of the role of the female adult. Many of the functions which the father might have fulfilled and many of those attributes which should have been ascribed to him were considered as properties of the mother. In addition, we have seen that the mother sometimes helped to create a false image of the father's role, which was seldom challenged or modified by the actual presence of the father.

In the case of Lucy, we found that the child had formed a concept of the male figure which represented him as an unpredictable being, one who could not be depended upon to appear in times of need, who had to be cajoled into providing for her needs by a show of helplessness or by the use of ruses, whom she must supervise or dominate in order to guard herself, somehow, against his repeated absences. She alternated these attitudes with some show of indirect hostility if she did not feel that she had succeeded in assuring the presence of her father or of me. Lucy clearly felt, as her behavior revealed, a general need for reassurance and attention from the male adult, and this need also colored her relationship with children of the male sex.

In Paul's case, the distortion of the male figure was more pronounced. The image he had formed for himself included only those qualities which represented stoical and "heroic" attitudes in men. It did not encompass nor allow for the expression of the many other human emotions which are an integral part of personality. This limitation of his concept of the male was reflected in Paul's behavior. We find him representing the male figure as a "ferocious warrior," as one who does not flinch under pain. Paul even disdains an expression of pain in an animal of the male sex. This attitude was further reflected in Paul's refusal to accept help from others or to be comforted by them, and by his constant efforts to assume a dominant role.

George is at almost the opposite end of the spectrum in his conception of the male figure. Through his own behavior and in his description of the father during projective play, we can see that he conceived of the masculine as a passive one. His own role as a boy is consequently somewhat of a mystery to him. George is a follower, a person who, to win the approval of others, must place himself in a subordinate position, and even then he shows uncertainty. But he also feared being dominated and resisted what he considered attempts to dominate him, alternating between submission and attempts at rebellion.

Barbara's concept of the male role was virtually a completely negative one. Her father's influence upon her was very much subordinate to that of her mother. Her mother's restrictive attitude toward life was, in fact, transferred to the child, thus limiting her acquaintance with and participation in those realms of experience her mother did not sanction.

One very serious consequence of an uneven distribution of parental influence is a general limitation of experience which prevents the child from realizing his full potential. The nature of this limitation is such that it will affect all areas of the child's behavior, directly or indirectly, and consequently weakens his ability to cope with his environment and tend to make him approach new situations with trepidation. The result is an uncertainty concerning himself and others and a desire to exclude those forces which challenge his preconceived values. Sometimes, the need for this exclusion is so powerful as to demand of the child either an almost superhuman effort or a barrier of complex mechanisms to shut out experiences and emotions which are foreign to his narrowed down concept of the world.

As to the uncertainty engendered in a child by this limitation of experience, we find in Lucy, for instance, a constant desire to test and re-test her position with regard to men and boys. She is uncertain not only of what the actions of others will be toward her but also of her own toward her peers. For George, the uncertainty is centered mainly on his own role as a boy, but it extends also to an uncertainty concerning his position among his peers and among adults.

Limitation of experience creates conflict by counterposing the child's natural desire to emerge into new realms of experience against a lack of confidence to do so.

Infrequent presence of the father or other male adults makes it extremely difficult for a boy to identify himself clearly with the masculine role. Although the child usually has some contact with male relatives and acquaintances, such more or less haphazard contact is seldom sufficient for him to form a correct image of the male role. The child needs a male relationship of greater consistency and depth if he is to form a correct and complete concept of the role which he is expected to play.

Infrequent presence of the father is as detrimental to a daughter as to a son. It limits her comprehension of the male role and robs her of opportunity to develop a satisfactory emotional tie with the paternal figure. It limits also the chances for the girl to develop her normal capacities for affection so necessary for the preparation of her future role as a woman. Finally, it limits her opportunity to evaluate her own position through comparison with that of males and so makes for a certain lack of clarity in her conception of her own role as a girl.

The conflict that is set up in a child through the limitations placed on his experience by too little contact with a male adult need not necessarily be unproductive. If conflict inhibits all action and paralyzes the emotions of the child, it is, of course, detrimental, for it cannot contribute to amelioration of the problem. If, however, conflict engenders effort, as it often does by the very intensity of the emotions it arouses, it may help the child to surmount a difficulty and can thus contribute to directing behavior into more positive channels. For example, when Paul's addiction to stoicism and denial of feelings came in conflict with my expression of concern and affection for him, the tension created by this conflict was at first expressed by fury and physical attacks on me. Later, however, it was redirected toward a breaking down of the barriers with which he had surrounded himself, which finally resulted in a release of dammed up emotions, and an ability to express them.

Conflict may also be resolved or ameliorated by the use of compensatory mechanisms which permit the child to enter an area of experience which he would otherwise completely avoid. Such mechanisms serve to reduce the "danger" of direct participation and also provide a less frightening way for the child to come to some kind of terms with unfamiliar experience. Barbara, for example could not bring herself to examine the rabbit when the other children were discussing sex characteristics, but she did examine the undersides of the fish in the aquarium. Although the conflict in Barbara was not completely resolved, it had helped initiate behavior which could eventually lead to the child's emergence from old behavior patterns and promote a healthier attitude toward areas of knowledge which she now tended to shun completely.

The resolution or amelioration of conflict evident in our case studies cannot be attributed to the possible productive nature of conflict alone. Since the emotional difficulties experienced by these children were mainly the result of their being too often deprived of the presence of male adults, the provision of consistent contact with a male adult in the nursery school was certainly an important factor in the resolution or amelioration of these difficulties. This is further substantiated by the case material, which shows that in each case improvement in behavior patterns was intimately allied with the child's attainment of a better understanding of the various aspects of the male role.

The last four of the eight cases discussed in this book deal with situations in which the presence of the father or other male adults is even further reduced, ranging from the case of a child who sees his father on alternate weekends to that of a child who has never seen or been in contact with her father at all. Here, too, of course, each case must be considered as unique in the sense that a particular set of circumstances have resulted in a pattern of effects peculiar to the specific case. Each case, however, can be considered as representative of situations which can tell us much about the detrimental effects that can be expected to accrue to any child who is deprived to a serious degree of the company of a father or of other male adults. Each case is also representance of a favorable change being effected in a child's emotional state and behavior pattern by the provision of consistent and sympathetic contact with an adult male.

The detrimental effects on the children involved in the last four of our cases are basically the same as those discussed in the cases of children from normal home backgrounds. They differ mainly in degree, appearing, as might be expected, in a more extreme form and having more profound impact upon the child's personality.

In each of these cases there is, first of all, an even greater distortion of the male role. The image of the father is obscured not only by infrequency or total lack of contact with him, but also by the need the child frequently feels to make up for this lack by the use of unproductive compensatory mechanisms or of fantasy constructions. Such attempts to fulfill a real need are, of course, detrimental to the child.

They are not founded upon a meaningful relationship nor can they provide any permanent solution to the problem. Often the child has no choice but to rely on these mechanisms (or to repress the need entirely). And, unless provided with a direct relationship with a male adult to help him satisfy his need, the danger exists that as his need increases he will more and more resort to these mechanisms. Thus, the greater the need and the less possibility of satisfying it by such methods the more distorted the object of these longings becomes.

In the four cases of children from normal home backgrounds, the distortion of the image of the male figure resulted in an unrealistic or too limited view of his functions and characteristics. In the cases of the four children from more disrupted family backgrounds, however, the distortion is even more extreme. The functions and characteristics of the male figure are more obscured, the person of the father being often veiled in wish-fulfilment fantasy, yearned for yet frequently feared, and seldom, if ever, partaking of human reality. The basic desires connected with the father often exceed the child's understanding of him.

The very force of the child's emotional need and the inability to fulfil it limit even further the possibility of creating a clear and realistic picture of the father. The child who lacks the benefit of close and consistent contact with the father is deprived of one of the most essential experiences in his life, the feeling of being loved and protected and the sense of belonging associated with a normal father-child relationship. If this deprivation is complete or nearly so and is prolonged enough, the child tends to lose his understanding of the initial need and to show a lack of comprehension of what he is actually deprived of, thus further decreasing the possibility of fulfilling his need realistically.

Judy, for example, interprets her deprivation mainly as a lowering of her status. Hear yearning for a father and her fantasy construction of one had little in common with the usual elements of this desire, namely the wish for closeness, protection, and love. She could not comprehend these elements since she had never experienced the significance of such a relationship. Tom, on the other hand, had had contact with his father for the first four years of his life, and although the father image is distorted, the boy has a desire for affection and closeness (even though repressed); he has at least a partial understanding of the implications of a father-child relationship. With Harriet and Philip the feelings for the father are surrounded by a great deal of emotional conflict, but here, too, is an awareness of the father-child relationship in terms of love and closeness, since they also have had experienced some actual contact of this sort.

Judy, having had no actual contact with a father, is not only lacking in positive feelings for him, she lacks all feelings for him, not even showing any of the negative feelings which, after all, are a part of the emotional responses of a child toward his parents. Tom, for example, does express such negative feelings about his father, interpreting his disappearance as an act of injustice; and he projects this resentment to other males. Harriet, too, shows negative as well as positive feelings about her father, as, for example, in her over-concern with his approval or disapproval which reveals her anxiety lest any disapproval on his part should further alienate his affections. In the case of Philip, the boy puts great emphasis on contacting his father and being with him; yet when he is confronted with him on his week-end visits, his feelings appear to be mixed and much tension is engendered by the visits.

In all four cases, the distortion of the male image affected the child's concepts of the male and female roles, and it affected the child's own concept of himself. As a result, the child's entire adjustment to his immediate world and his conception of his future role became adversely affected. Thus, Harriet misinterprets her own role and that of her parents as well. To compensate for her lack of closeness with her father, she has had to distort his role in such a way as to allow her to believe that she can effect his return by retaining the established order that reigned before his departure. As a result, she assigns to herself powers beyond her actual function as a child, which in turn distorts her concept of the roles of her parents. In her attempt to control factors in their lives which no one could any longer control, she loses practically all sense of perspective of a parent-child relationship. Her desire to create an equilibrium in a home where no equilibrium is possible at the moment inevitably leads her to fabricate situations and powers which would create such equilibrium, and this tends further to distort her picture of her parents, her relationship with them, and her concept of her own functions.

In the case of Philip, the need to satisfy a desire for harmony in the home, which in reality was unattainable, results in mechanisms designed to obtain the presence of the father without the attending censure of the mother. This behavior then brings about conflict in the boy and a distortion of his concept of both parents. The father, and attainment of his presence, are cloaked in abstractions and in fantasies, and all references to him are for the most part indirect. The boy shows very little sense of security in his portrayal of his father or in his indirect references to him. His mother is considered as a person from whom feelings concerning a father must be carefully hidden, with a resulting distortion of the female figure also.

In the case of Tom, the child sees his father as a perpetrator of injustice, yet he also yearns for him. The child's resentment of his dead father stems partially from his incomplete understanding of the meaning of death. The boy's relationship with his mother has also been adversely affected; he feels that he has to protect her from other men, and that he also must protect himself from having to share her affection, which is now the only affection he can allow himself. His misorientation toward his father results also in a distortion of his conception of other men and of his own role as a member of the male sex.

Judy's more extreme distortion of the male role leads to an imaginary father with unrealistic qualities. The effect it has on her concept of self is reflected in the sense of inadequacy which she feels as a result of his absence and the uncertainty which arises from this feeling in her dealings with other children and with adults. Her almost complete lack of understanding of what it means for a daughter to have the love and affection of a father also distorts her comprehension of the female role, a fact which could have an unfortunate influence on her ability to accept her role as a woman in later life.

No one set of factors determining behavior can be affected without affect upon the whole personality structure. It is, therefore, not surprising that a distortion in one area of personality results in repercussions of this distortion in many other areas of a child's adjustment to the world around him.

Children who are completely, or nearly completely deprived of the father's presence do indeed suffer a serious limitation of experience. There is, of course, the usual limitation caused by being deprived of the father's presence. In addition, the increased seriousness of this deprivation is likely to result in greater tension being set up in the child. His efforts to cope with this tension become correspondingly more intense, to a point where they threaten to become his sole preoccupation. Consequently, the child feels little inclination to desert his preoccupation in favor of trying new experiences or exploring new areas which, in turn, might aid him in solving his problem. The child's involvement with the conflict demands much of his psychic energy, leaving him little force to expend on efforts to explore his environment or to develop the full potential of any relationship or activity.

Philip, for example, is unable to participate in any area not directly connected with his particular preoccupation. While he is in the throes of his conflict he is completely isolated from the group and from new experiences. This limitation is seen again in the case of Harriet: her preoccupation with order prevents her from entering new situations. Even those areas of play she seems to enjoy are often eschewed in favor of attempts to relieve her tension over her father's absence. The limitation in Tom's experience manifests itself in his inability to maintain interest in any activity and in the erratic nature of his personal relationships. In addition, he strives to limit his contacts with men, even attempting to exclude them from his presence. Judy's experience with children is limited because of her preoccupation with the inadequacy of her family background compared with that of others. Her relationships with them are further limited because her extensive use of fantasy tends to make her operate on a plain that is too unreal to be long interesting to the others. As a result, she finds herself on the periphery of the group. With Judy, as with the other three children, the desire to reach an emotional equilibrium, to relieve the conflict by fulfilling the need which engendered it, is always present; but the impossibility of doing so unaided elicits constant recapitulation of the problem and forces the child to dwell on it almost exclusively.

Children who at one time enjoyed a complete and satisfactory home structure and who are later faced with disharmony or with an incomplete family life often attempt to conjure up the past and even treat it as if it were still the real situation. Fantasies of various sorts are constructed, and habits, attitudes, and activities of the happier past are conjured up to cope with or to escape from present conflicts. The child feels that if he can regain at least some part of a happier past, somehow, the state of affairs obtaining at the time will return. Thus we see the rise of magical practices, a representative portion of a situation being re-enacted to conjure up the appearance of the situation in its entirety and in its original form.[1]

At the beginning of the school year and at periods of great tension, several of the children resorted to fantasy activities, often of a sort that had obvious connections with earlier stages of their lives. Harriet's preoccupation with earlier and happier order of things is most clearly seen in her refusal to have any of the furniture in her room changed,

---

[1] Jean Piaget has also noted (*The Child's Conception of the World*, p. 133) that children at times perform some action or mental operation, which they believe to have an influence or power over some particular event they either wish for or fear. The original gestures tend to become symbolic, that is, mere signs, detached from their original content.

a preoccupation which had arisen only after the disruption of her home. The child gave evidence of anxiety lest any disturbance of the established order of things alienate her male teacher or further alienate her father. Philip also resorted to activities which were liked with a period in his earlier life; he resorted to them partly because they represented a happier stage of experience than the present, and also because they did not require difficult new adjustments. He relied on sewing, books, and the company of adults, each of which, being related to familiar experiences in the past, tended to protect him from acknowledgment of his present difficult position. So, too, with Tom. The one activity which at the beginning of the school year allowed him to feel relatively at peace was connected with the past, when his family circle was complete.

The referral to the past is not something upon which the child can build constructively. It is not a part of the learning process, but a method of escaping the tensions presented by the reality. It tends to create a static frame of reference within the child. It restrains him from approaching his problems in a more constructive way and from entering into new experiences. Unless the child is provided with a more constructive way of relieving tension or fulfilling his needs, he has little opportunity to emerge from this detrimental pattern of behavior.

In every case, a decided change was brought about through the opportunity provided the children to make contact with a male adult. Side by side with those forces which were detrimental to optimum development there existed a desire to fulfil basic needs and to modify unsatisfying behavior. Since most of their difficulties were the result of conflicting forces engendered by insufficient con-

tact with the father, the provision of contact with a male
adult who was not heir to these conflicting forces permitted
the children to establish a sound and much-needed relationship that could in turn permit them access to a constructive
approach to their problem.

Harriet's anxiety over alienating the affections of her
father or other men was lessened through the realization
that she could be consistently accepted by a male adult, and
she was able to devote herself to a wider range of experiences
and consequently achieve better adjustment. For Philip,
the constant reassurance of my presence, without the excessive demands which his relationship with his father put
upon him, helped him to redirect some of the energy he
had used in his futile attempts to solve his predicament
toward a contact from which he could gain some real
satisfaction. Although the progress in his behavior was
slowed by the great emotional difficulties under which he
labored, it clearly indicated that a constructive change was
in process. Tom's opportunity to relate to a male adult was
of great importance. He had previously been able to express
only one side of his feelings concerning men, and his distorted view was coupled with difficulty in fully accepting his
own sex role, which he interpreted in a negative fashion. By
constant contact with a male adult, he was able to modify
his attitudes of mistrust and hostility and to express his
desire for closeness and affection, which had until then remained repressed. For Judy, who lacked a basic experience
of a father-child relationship and showed a tendency to
deal with it in terms of a completely unrealistic involvement,
my presence was perhaps of the greatest importance of all.
It enabled her to supplant the phantom-father she had
created with a series of real-life experiences, explorations,

and close contacts. As a result, she arrived at those conceptions which could give her the basis of understanding she
needed as a vital part of her development and which she
had so completely lacked before.

TOPICS FOR DISCUSSION

Chapter 11 *The Missing Male*
1. How important is it for a teacher, social worker, etc. to have
   extensive data on a child before any hypotheses are raised in
   regard to the meaning of a child's behavior?

Father and Child:
The Complexes

TWO pertinent and interrelated problems deserve to be treated in greater detail than the preceding chapters have permitted: namely, the Oedipus complex, which has appeared recurrently in the reactions of the children studied, and the psychological process of identification on the part of the child with his parents and other important adults.

The Oedipus complex is directly relevant, since it manifests itself during the period of early childhood and involves the father as one of the principal personages. But although it will be necessary to give a brief general view of the Oedipal situation, we shall consider it only as it applies to our study. The object will be to try to show how its effects may be channelled so that the child may be helped to overcome the emotional difficulties which arise at this period in his life.

To begin with, one must realize that each of the component parts of the Oedipal triangle (father, mother, and child) contributes to its complexity. The mother is the child's first object of love and of identification. He receives her undivided attention in infancy. As he grows older and can function more independently, he is expected to give up some of his exclusive claims upon her and share her affection with the father. This situation is difficult for the child to accept and he begins to see his father as an obstacle and as a threat to the fulfilment of his desires. He becomes resentful and hostile toward the father, while at the same time he admires, loves, and in part identifies with him. These opposing impulses make for ambivalent feelings and create additional conflict in the child which is heightened by feelings of guilt over his hostility and fear of possible retaliation by the father.

The Oedipus conflict is resolved when the child begins to accept his role in the family group and realizes that his father is the authority figure whose functions he cannot take over, but with whom he can identify and whose masculine behavior he can emulate. This process is aided by the approval the child may receive for giving up the desire to shut out the father and for incorporating the male concepts symbolized by him. The resolution of the conflict makes the child more independent of his mother, which in turn enables him to develop normally and later to transfer his love for her to other female figures.[1]

The temporarily insoluble nature of the Oedipus conflict, however, leaves the child in difficult straits, and it is not until he is able either to sublimate his desires or redirect his

[1] The classic description of the Oedipus complex as given by Freud has been qualified by the fact that the father in our society is not as much of a punitive, authoritarian figure as was the Germanic prototype. Also, today we are less likely to consider the child as a miniature adult, and consequently there exists greater parental understanding and a lessening in the intensity of the struggle between father and child.

energies into acceptable channels (or to transfer his feelings to other adults, thus diluting the strength of this essentially intra-familial conflict), that he is able to achieve a success-ful resolution of the complex. And it is at this point that the present investigation is particularly relevant, for the child can be helped in some measure to achieve this resolution by being given the opportunity to redirect some of the am-bivalent and conflicting feelings for his father to an adult of the male sex who is not involved in the familial constellation and is therefore outside the conflict area.

As a representative of the male figure, such a man may allow the child to establish a relationship with him in which less tension arises but from which the child can nevertheless derive the fulfilment of those needs which the struggle with the father has momentarily made impossible for him to satisfy. The love and warmth the child originally felt for the father, for example, which at the moment may be out-weighed by hostility, can find their object in another male adult; similarly, the hostility which the child may be forced to repress out of fear of the retaliating father may find safer expression toward an adult other than the father; and outside of the familial environment the child can be helped toward a more objective and less emotionally charged out-look on the situation. The relationship thus established can be expected to do more than reduce the tension of the con-flict; it may at a later date, when the Oedipus problem has diminished, permit the child to arrive at a better-balanced and more positive view of the father and of the male figure in general. Otherwise, the hostility which the child feels for the father and the tremendous anxieties it gives rise to within him may be repressed because of fear, the original hostility may remain buried, and consequently remain connected with the father figure in later years, with resultant harm to emotional growth.

Such efforts to lessen the tensions of the Oedipus situation may be of even greater significance in cases (such as those of Philip and Tom) where the father has absented himself or has died at a time when the conflicts regarding him can be expected to be in their active state. There then exists a greater risk than usual, of the Oedipus complex being arrested in its development, with consequent detrimental effects on the child's normal growth. The child's whole psychosexual development may be affected. The boy, for example, may remain attached to the mother, fail to develop proper masculinity concepts, and decline to accept the male role. Sometimes, when other contributing factors are present (and especially if the father has left the familial scene in the midst of the Oedipal conflict and thus lessened the chances of its being resolved in the normal course of events) sexual deviance may ensue.

The Electra complex, in which for the girl the father becomes the love-object and the mother the obstacle between her and the father, gives rise to the same conflict. The daughter whose father is absent from the home has neither the opportunity to establish the attachment for the father which is a necessary part of development nor the opportunity of properly resolving the resultant conflict. She may, as a result fail to develop her feminine role; and, under such circumstances, the danger of psycho-sexual misorientation may be as great for the female as for the male. Here again, the presence of a male adult, one outside the familial setting, may provide a relationship that will at least partially satisfy the child's emotional needs that have been temporarily thwarted within the family. And, as with the male child, the consistent presence of an adult male may be most important when a daughter is deprived of sufficient contact with her father.

It is, in short, of the greatest importance that a child be provided with a relationship with a male adult which will permit him to experience and help him eventually resolve these developing emotional conflicts. By virtue of a continuous relationship of this kind, the child can be helped to act out those problems for which the family can provide either no adequate outlet (as is often the case with children who come from normal homes) or none at all (as in the case of children whose father is too much or completely absent from the home scene).

The progressive changes in Tom's behavior, for example, clearly reflect the development of the Oedipal situation and its partial resolution. Tom showed at first, it will be remembered, an indirectly expressed resentment toward me which seemed to extend to other male adults as well, notably the man his mother thought of marrying. The resentment became especially pronounced when Tom felt that my presence was an obstacle to his receiving his mother's undivided attention or the attentions of the woman teacher. Later he was able to manifest his hostility toward me in a more direct and outward manner. Then, finally, he developed warmth and affection for me and a better attitude toward his dead father and showed less desire to keep the attentions of his mother and the woman teacher centered exclusively upon himself.

The second problem to be considered here in greater detail is that of identification of the child with his parents and other important adults.

For the young child, the parental figures provide, or should provide, satisfactory object for identification. This identification is of the greatest importance as a basis for later development and for the acceptance of the child's proper sex-role. It is a necessity not only for the child's future role in his society, but also for the establishment of satisfactory adult emotional relationships. Through the process of identification the child learns to incorporate concepts of reality outside of himself, the attitudes and behavior patterns of others, and the mores of his culture group in general. As a result, his rational self develops, and the process of emotional and intellectual growth is furthered.

The father is important in furnishing emotional contact for his daughter and in being an object of identification for his son so that he may surmount the Oedipal conflict and accept the male role. The father balances the feminine influence of the mother, thus giving both the boy and the girl a better and more complete view of their respective sex-roles. The complementary action of both parents provides the best basis for familial education and proper development.

When one considers the vital nature of the contribution made by each of the parents in becoming an object of identification for the child, one realizes once again, the seriousness of the situation in which one parent is not present in the home (or at least not to a sufficient degree) to furnish a vivid enough model for the child. We have seen that this condition exists in broken and incomplete homes, and also, to some extent, in the normal homes of present-day industrial society. We have noted the difficulties children from such home have experienced in making proper identification, and we have seen identification being based on a one-sided and contorted conception. We have also seen how absence of one of the major figures on the familial scene causes a damaging experiential gap, and we know that it may, in severe cases, constitute the basis for future complexes.

The child coming from a broken home will in most cases have greater difficulty in making proper identification and incorporating realistic parental images than will the child from a home in which the presence of one of the parents is merely reduced. These difficulties may manifest themselves in fantasy images, fictitious parents, and the like. Such unrealistic expression clearly indicates that the emotional needs of the child have not been properly satisfied. It is not until another adult can take over some of the functions of the missing or seldom-present parent that the child begins to arrive at a point where a balanced conception of reality is made possible. Even for the child whose contact with both parents is fairly adequate, a relationship with another important adult outside of the family circle is of great value for the development of less subjective views. Such contacts, by exposing him to the views of others, can broaden the child's perceptions, help him to overcome biased or limited concepts, and aid him to achieve a more rational orientation. This is a necessary and valuable step in the child's development, since in fostering objectivity and helping the child realize that his own perceptions are not absolute, it forms the basis for the future expansion of his emotional and intellectual powers. The children whose cases we have been concerned with in this study usually arrived on the school scene with a series of subjective, limited, and often biased opinions about men. It was not until the effects of socialization provided by the school setting had taken hold and they had gained insight and experience through contact with a male adult outside the family environment that their conceptions and attitudes grew broader, better balanced, and more realistic.

Topics for Discussion

Chapter 12 *Father and Child*

1. Compare the modern American father to the Germanic father Freud described.
2. Is the modern American woman different than her grandmother? How has this change in the role of women influenced the child's image of his parents?
3. Is it easier for girls to identify with their mothers than it is for boys to identify with their fathers?

Some Recommendations

THIS study has demonstrated the great importance of male influence for the young child and the problems posed by the fact that in our society the child is too often not adequately exposed to it in his home. It has also shown the constructive results which can be achieved when greater male influence is supplied in the life of the child. The question then is how best to ameliorate the conditions which now exist, within and outside the family, that militate against such influence.

Though no two family situations are the same, certain general suggestions can be offered to lessen the effects of infrequent male presence. These suggestions are, of course, meant to serve simply as a guide. They may be modified according to a family's particular needs and supplemented by other constructive measures. In general, however, a dual approach to the problem is probably most effective; first, additional male influence should be provided within the family circle when the situation warrants. Secondly, various social institutions should make a serious effort to supply male influence for the child outside the family circle.

Let us first consider how the child may be adequately exposed to male as well as female influence in the average family where both parents are present. The following recommendations may seem to belabor the obvious, but the obvious is sometimes forgotten:

The father should participate whenever possible in the child's experiences and interests; he should become involved in his world and encourage a warm emotional relationship. He should try to be guide, protector, friend, and authority; but, above all, he should try to come alive to the child as a whole person, and not keep part of his personality aloof.

The mother can be of great help in reinforcing the father's place in the family by attributing important functions to him, and sharing with him projects and decisions that concern the child. When the father is absent from the home during work hours, she can bring him into the child's life through references to him and his activities. Various books (some of which are listed in the Appendix) can be given the child to help him understand the activities of fathers at work and the male role in general, as well as illustrate to the child how men behave and think. It is most important that the emotional climate surrounding any attempt to help the child understand his parents be warm and natural and that the parents not merely feed information to the child but be sincerely interested in sharing their lives with him.

The parents can also encourage male relatives and friends to become a part of the life of the child. Older brothers can also help to broaden and further clarify the child's conceptions of masculine attitudes, values, interests and activities.

To supply adequate male influence for the child from a home in which the father is absent or very rarely present is a somewhat more difficult problem. Any possibility for a child to have a prolonged and satisfying relationship with a male adult relative, teacher, or family friend should be exploited. The child should be given the opportunity to visit other homes where both parents are present so that he may receive a more realistic and better-balanced picture of home-life. Male group-workers in community centers, camp counselors, and so on, can greatly contribute to the child's understanding and emotional enrichment, especially since the child's enjoyment of the recreational activities often provided by these people contributes to the constructive nature of the relationship and facilitates the child's identification with them.

Emotional maturity on the part of the divorced or separated parent who is entrusted with care of the child is important if the child is to develop a healthy attitude. Although a mother may have found it difficult to continue living with her husband, she should try not to generalize her resentment or disillusionment and so give the child a prejudiced view of the male sex. It is equally important for the father, who may see the child once in a while, not to influence him against the mother or other female adults. The causes behind the family schism should be interpreted to the child according to his emotional and mental maturity, and in an atmosphere of trust and affection.

In the case of the death of the father, the child, besides being brought into prolonged contact with other male adults when possible, should be encouraged to talk freely about the deceased and to express his feelings, whether of love, regret or resentment. A parent substitute should be provided for the child as soon as feasible, and the remaining parent should be careful not to make the child a surrogate for the deceased spouse.

If the home however, cannot provide the proper amelioration or if its measures need to be supplemented, the nursery school can provide the very young child with the male influence which may be lacking in the home. *If the nursery school is to be instrumental, however, in alleviating the problem of the absent father, its present character must be changed by the inclusion of men as well as women on its staff.* At present it tends to perpetuate the detrimental pattern. By excluding men as teachers of the pre-school child, it limits the child's perspective and his chances of obtaining a well-balanced view of the society he is beginning to enter. The author urgently suggests this necessary change in the present nursery school set-up to provide a setting in which men and women participate equally. Such a change would enhance the already great value of the nursery school and aid it to carry out even more meaningfully the functions it now fulfills. It would be a change in the direction of enabling education to achieve one of its most vital goals, that of bringing the child into real-life contact with all the important components of his society.

It may be asked why it is of such import to supplement male presence in the life of the child, at precisely *this* stage in his development (although it is of course vital at all ages) and why this task should not be postponed until a later date. First, the child at the age at which he usually enters nursery school is no longer mainly absorbed in the close relationship with his mother which is characteristic of the early years of infancy. His father has begun to take on greater significance and the child is now ready to profit more fully from a relationship with him. But, as we have seen, incidence of presence in the home unfortunately does not increase with the child's increased need of him. As it is the task of the good school to provide the child with an environment which puts within his reach all those experiences which will best contribute to furthering his development, it should, at the stage at which the father becomes important, provide the child with a male adult to whom he can relate and who can, to some extent, make up for a father's infrequent presence in the home.

The adult representative of the female figure is already provided for in the structure of the nursery school. It now remains to balance this structure. Since the nursery school forms an important link between early years of infancy spent mostly in the home and later expansion into the societal and cultural milieu, it should use every possible means to supplement the functions of the family as it helps prepare the child to understand the outside world. (It is equally true, of course, that more men teachers should be employed at the elementary school level.)

How can such a change be effected? Persuasion and action are necessary. Obviously the idea must first have the support of people in the fields of psychology and education. Through them, it can reach the policy makers of educational institutions who can provide the practical application by making the appropriate changes in their staffs. Also, every effort should be made, through parent-teacher meetings and other agencies, to inform parents of the benefits and advantages of the new order. At the same time, the plan must be presented persuasively to teacher-trainees to encourage men to enter the field and to help remove the prejudices which often deter them from doing so. The final acceptance of the idea depends, however, on the support of the public. It is they, parents and prospective parents, who must be persuaded of the important role of the male in nursery and elementary schools.

Once the problem is understood and analyzed, the first step towards its solution has been taken. When the sincere desire exists to alter a state of affairs which may be detrimental to the child, the means will certainly be found to do so.

TOPICS FOR DISCUSSION

Chapter 13 *Some Recommendations*
1. Why have men hesitated to work as teachers with very young children?
2. There was a time in the history of our country when men played an almost exclusive role in educating the young child. What factors do you suggest have caused this situation to be so drastically altered today?
3. If you were asked to select male and female teachers for a kindergarten set-up what personality characteristics would you feel it advisable to consider?

Bibliography

Chapter 1

Ausubel, D. P., *Theory and Problems of Child Development,* Grune and Stratton, New York, 1958.

Bach, G. R., "Father-Fantasies and Father-Typing in Father-Separated Children," *Child Development,* Vol. 17, 1946, pp. 63-80.

Baldwin, A. L., *Behavior and Development in Childhood,* Dryden, New York, 1955.

Benedek, T., "The Emotional Structure of the Family," In: *The Family: Its Functions and Destiny,* Science of Culture Series, Vol. V, Harper Brothers, New York, 1949.

Benedict, R., "The Family: Genus Americanus," In: *The Family: Its Functions and Destiny,* Science of Culture Series, Vol. V, Harper Brothers, New York, 1949.

Benjamin, Z., *Emotional Problems of Childhood,* University of London Press, London, 1948.

Bergeron, M., "Le premier âge," *L'Ecole des Parents,* No. 3, January, 1955, pp. 3-13.

Bowlby, J., "The Study and Reduction of Group Tensions in the Family," *Human Relations,* Vol. II, No. 2, April, 1949, pp. 123-128.

Burlingham, D. and Freud, A., *Enfants sans famille,* Presses Universitaires de France, Paris, 1949.

Cattell, R. B., *Personality,* McGraw Hill, New York, 1950.

Chateau, J., *L'enfant et le jeu,* Editions du Scarabée, Paris, 1950.

Cook, L. A. and Cook, E., *Sociological Approach to Education,* McGraw-Hill, New York, 1950.

Debesse, M., "Le sentiment paternel dans la psychologie masculine," *L'Ecole des Parents,* No. 2, December, 1953, pp. 4-14.

Duvall, E. M., "Conceptions of Parenthood," *American Journal of Sociology,* No. 52, 1946, pp. 193-203.

Erikson, E., *Childhood and Society,* W. W. Norton, New York, 1950.

Gardner, P. L., "A Survey of the Attitudes and Activities of Fathers," *Journal of Genetic Psychology,* No. 63, 1943, pp. 15-53.

———, "An Analysis of Children's Attitudes Toward Fathers," *Journal of Genetic Psychology,* No. 70, 1947, pp. 3-28.

Gesell, A. and Ilg, F., *Infant and Child in the Culture of Today,* Harper Brothers, New York, 1943.

———, *The Child From Five to Ten,* Harper Brothers, New York, 1946.

Henry, J. and Warson, S., "Family Structure and Psychic Development," *American Journal of Orthopsychiatry,* Vol. 21, January, 1951, pp. 59-73.

Isaacs, S., *Parents et enfants. Leurs difficultés quotidiennes,* Presses Universitaires de France, Paris, 1952.

Jung, C. G., *Conflits de l'âme enfantine. La rumeur. L'influence du père,* Editions Montaigne, Paris, 1935.

Kanner, L., *Child Psychiatry,* Charles C Thomas, Springfield, Illinois, 1949.

Klineberg, O., "The Father's Role—Now and in the Past," *Child Study Association of America,* Vol. 34, No. 3, Summer, 1957, pp. 12-18.

Lacan, J. M., "Le complexe, facteur concret de la psychologie familiale," In: *La Vie Mentale,* Vol. VIII/I, Section A., Société de Gestion de l'Encyclopédie Française, Paris, March, 1938.

La Piere, R. T. and Farnsworth, P., *Social Psychology,* McGraw Hill, New York, 1949.

Lerner, E., *Constraint Areas and the Moral Judgment of Children,* Banta, Menasha, Wisconsin, 1937.

Levinger, L. and Murphy, L. B., "Implications of the Social Sense for the Education of Young Children," *Yearbook of National Social Studies in Education,* Part II, 1947, pp. 15-43.

Meltzer, H., "Sex Differences in Children's Attitudes to Parents," *Journal of Genetic Psychology,* No. 62, 1943, pp. 311-326.

Mott, S. M., "Concept of Mother—A Study of Four and Five Year Old Children," *Child Development,* No. 25, 1954, pp. 99-106.

————, "Mother-Father Preference," *Character and Personality,* No. 5, 1937, pp. 302-304.

Nimkoff, M. F., "The Child's Preference for Mother or Father," *American Sociological Review,* No. 7, 1942, pp. 517-524.

Parsons, T., "Age and Sex in the Social Structure of the United States," *American Sociological Review,* No. 7, 1942, pp. 604-616.

————, "The Social Structure of the Family," In: *The Family: Its Functions and Destiny,* Science of Culture Series, Vol. V, Harper Brothers, New York, 1949.

Plant, J. S., *Personality and the Cultural Pattern,* The Commonwealth Fund, University of Oxford Press, London, 1937.

Porot, M., *L'enfant et les relations familiales,* Presses Universitaires de France, Paris, 1954.

Rabban, M., "Sex Role Identification in Young Children in Two Diverse Social Groups," *Genetic Psychology Monographs,* No. 4, 1950, pp. 81-158.

Roff, M., "Intra-Family Resemblances in Personality Characteristics," *Journal of Psychology,* No. 30, 1950, pp. 199-227.

Sears, P. S., "Doll-Play Aggression in Normal Young Children: Influence of Sex, Age, Sibling Status, Father's Absence," *Psychological Monographs,* Vol. 65, No. 5, 1951, pp. 1-43.

Sears, R., Macoby, E. and Levin, H., *Patterns of Child Rearing,* Row Peterson and Company, Illinois, 1957.

Sears, R., Pintler, M. and Sears, P. S., "Effects of Father-Separation on Pre-school Children's Doll-Play Aggression," *Child Development,* Vol. 17, No. 4, December, 1946, pp. 219-243.

Seward, G. H., *Sex and the Social Order,* McGraw Hill, New York, 1946.

Simpson, M., *Parent Preference of Young Children,* Teachers' College, Columbia University, New York, 1935.

Tasch, R. J., "The Role of the Father in the Family," *Journal of Experimental Education,* No. 20, 1952, pp. 319-361.

Truxal, A. G. and Merrill, F. E., *The Family in American Culture,* Prentice Hall, New York, 1947.

Wicks, F. G., "Childhood Problems As Seen From the Analytic Psychology of C. G. Jung," In: *Handbook of Child Guidance,* Childcare Publications, New York, 1947, pp. 723-733.

Zimmerman, C. C., *The Family of Tomorrow,* Harper Brothers, New York, 1949.

Chapter 2

Anderson, H. and Anderson, G., *An Introduction to Projective Techniques,* Prentice Hall, New York, 1951.

Bossard, J. S., *Parent and Child Studies in Family Breakdown,* University of Pennsylvania Press, Philadelphia, 1953.

Bowlby, A. (Ed.), "Abnormal Influences on the Psychology of the Child," In: *The Influence of Home and Community on Children Under 13 Years of Age Towards World Understanding,* Unesco Publications, Paris, 1949.

Bowlby, J., "The Study and Reduction of Group Tensions in the Family," *Human Relations,* Vol. II, No. 2, April, 1949, pp. 123-128.

Claparède, E., *Le développement mental,* Delachaux et Niestlé, S. A., Neuchâtel, Suisse, 1946.

Cordelier, S., *Les enfants de la discorde,* Les Editions Sociales Françaises, Paris, 1954.

Dantziger, D., "Le théâtre et l'éducation. Point de départ de l'essai du jeu dramatique," In: *Archives Belges des Sciences de l'Education,* Vol. II, No. 2, Uccle, Belgium, 1936, pp. 127-134.

Dewey, J., *Experience and Education,* Macmillan Company, New York, 1953.

Favez-Boutonnier, J., "Le rôle de la famille dans la prophylaxie des troubles mentaux," *Bulletin de Psychologie,* No. 5, February, 1954, pp. 264-267.

Frank, L. K., *Projective Methods,* C. C. Thomas, Springfield, Illinois, 1948.

Finch, H. M., "Young Children's Concept of Parent Roles," *Journal of Home Economics,* No. 47, 1955, pp. 99-103.

Heuyer, G., "Psychopathologie de l'enfant victime de la guerre," *Sauvegarde,* January, 1948, pp. 3-46.

Jackson, L. and Todd, K. M., *Child Treatment and the Therapy of Play,* Methuen and Company, London, 1946.

Kodlin, D. and Donovan, J. T., "An Appraisal of the Longitudinal Approach to Studies in Growth and Development," *Monograph of Social Research in Child Development,* Vol. 67, No. 1, 1958, pp. 1-47.

Lacan, J. M., "Les complexes familiaux en pathologie," In: *La Vie Mentale,* Vol. VIII/II, Société de Gestion de l'Encyclopédie Française, Paris, March, 1938.

La Piere, T. and Farnsworth, P., *Social Psychology,* McGraw Hill, New York, 1949.

Menut, G. C., *La dissociation familiale et les troubles du caractère chez l'enfant,* Editions Familiales de France, Paris, 1944.

Munn, N. L., *Psychology. The Fundamentals of Human Adjustment,* George Harrap, London, 1954.

Murphy, G., *An Introduction to Psychology,* Harper Brothers, New York, 1951.

Olson, W. C., "Measurement of Character," In: *Encyclopedia of Educational Research,* The Macmillan Company, New York, 1950.

Piaget, J., "Le jeu et l'hygiène mentale de l'enfance," In: *L'hygiène mentale des enfants et des adolescents,* Delachaux et Niestlé, S. A., Neuchâtel and Paris, 1943.

Simpson, M., *Parent Preference of Young Children,* Teachers' College, Columbia University, New York, 1935.

Sirjamaki, J., *The American Family in the Twentieth Century,* Harvard University Press, Cambridge, Massachusetts, 1953.

Stolz, L. M. and Collaborators, *Father Relations of War-Born Children,* Stanford University Press, Stanford, 1954.

Teicher, J. D., *Your Child and His Problems,* Little, Brown and Company, Boston, 1953.

Truxal, A. G. and Merrill, F. E., *The Family in American Culture,* Prentice Hall, New York, 1947.

Chapter 11

Aberle, D. F. and Naegele, K. D., "Middle Class Fathers' Occupational Role and Attitudes Toward Children," *American Journal of Orthopsychiatry,* No. 22, 1952, pp. 366-378.

Lewin, K., "Environmental Forces in Child Behavior," In: *A Handbook of Child Psychology,* Clark University Press, Worcester, Massachusetts, 1951.

Piaget, J., *The Child's Conception of the World,* Routledge and Kegan Paul, London, 1951.

Chapter 12

Aberle, D. F. and Naegele, K. D., "Middle Class Fathers' Occupational Role and Attitudes Toward Children," *American Journal of Orthopsychiatry,* No. 22, 1952, pp. 366-378.

Ausubel, D. P., *Theory and Problems of Child Development,* Grune and Stratton, New York, 1958.

Balint, A., *The Early Years of Life,* Basic Books Incorporated, New York, 1954.

Blum, G. S., *Psychoanalytic Theories of Personality,* McGraw Hill, New York, 1953.

Burlingham, D. and Freud, A., *Enfants sans famille,* Presses Universitaires de France, Paris, 1949.

Conn, J. H., "Children's Reactions to the Discovery of Genital Differences," *American Journal of Orthopsychiatry,* No. 10, 1940, pp. 747-755.

Davis, A., "Child Training in Social Class," In: *Child Behavior and Development* (Eds.: Barker, Kounin and Wright), McGraw Hill, New York, 1943, pp. 607-620.

Debesse, M., "Le sentiment paternel dans la psychologie masculine," *L'Ecole des Parents,* No. 2, December, 1953, pp. 4-14.

Dillon, M. S., "Attitudes of Children Toward Their Own Bodies and Those of Other Children," *Child Development,* No. 5, 1934, pp. 165-176.

English, S. O. and Pearson, G. H., *Common Neuroses in Children and Adults,* W. W. Norton and Company, New York, 1937.

Fenichel, O., *The Psychoanalytic Theory of Neuroses,* W. W. Norton and Company, New York, 1945.

Freud, S., *Collected Papers,* Vol. II, Hogarth Press, London, 1950.

————, *New Introductory Lectures on Psycho-Analysis,* W. W. Norton and Company, New York, 1953.

Finch, H. M., "Young Children's Concept of Parent Roles," *Journal of Home Economics,* 1955, No. 47, pp. 99-103.

Honzik, M. P., "Sex Differences in the Occurrence of Materials in the Play Constructions of Pre-Adolescents," *Child Development,* No. 22, 1951, pp. 15-35.

Joseph, H. and Zern, G., *The Emotional Problems of Children,* Crown Publishers Incorporated, New York, 1954.

Kagan, J., "The Child's Perception of the Parent," In: *The Child: A Book of Readings* (Eds.: Seidman, Jerome), Rinehart and Company, New York, 1958.

Kitay, P. M., "A Comparison of the Sexes in Their Attitudes

and Beliefs About Women: A Study of Prestige Groups," *Sociometry,* No. 3, 1940, pp. 399-407.

Lacan, J. M., "Le complexe, facteur concret de la psychologie familiale," In: *La Vie Mentale, Vol.* VIII/I, Société de Gestion de l'Encyclopédie Française, Paris, March, 1938.

Levy, R. A., "The Father in the Home," In: *Emotional Problems of Childhood,* by Z. Benjamin, University of London Press, London, 1948.

Lippman, H. S., *Treatment of the Child in Emotional Conflict,* The Blakiston Division, McGraw-Hill, New York, 1956.

Marcault, J. E., "Ce que la psychanalyse peut apporter au caractère de l'enfant," *Collection: La psychologie de l'enfant de 7 à 14 ans,* Cahiers de Pédagogie Moderne, Paris, 1937, pp. 31-36.

Mauco, G., "Les relations de l'écolier et du maître," *L'Ecole des Parents,* No. 7, May, 1953, pp. 17-26.

Mueller, D. D., "Parental Domination: Its Influence on Child Guidance Results," *Smith College Studies of Social Work,* No. 15, 1945, pp. 184-215.

Murphy, G., Murphy, L. B. and Newcomb, T. M., *Experimental Social Psychology,* Harper Brothers, New York, 1937.

Piaget, J., *The Child's Conception of Physical Causality,* Routledge and Kegan Paul, London, 1951.

Porot, M., *L'enfant et les relations familiales,* Presses Universitaires de France, Paris, 1954.

Radke, M. J., "The Relation of Parental Authority to Children's Behavior and Attitudes," *University of Minnesota Institute of Child Welfare Monographs,* No. 22, 1946, pp. 1-33.

Redl, F. and Wattenberg, W. W., *Mental Hygiene in Teaching,* Harcourt, Brace and Company, New York, 1951.

Robin, G., *Les haines familiales,* Gallimard, Paris, 1926.

Roff, M., "Intra-Family Resemblances in Personality Characteristics," *Journal of Psychology,* No. 30, 1950, pp. 199-227.

Sears, R., Macoby, E. and Levin, H., *Patterns of Child Rearing,* Row Peterson and Company, Illinois, 1957.

Subes, J., "Hypothèse sur l'enfance," *Enfance,* No. 1, 1952, pp. 48-75.

Tasch, R. J., "The Role of the Father in the Family," *Journal of Experimental Education,* No. 20, 1952, pp. 319-361.

Thompson, G. G., *Child Psychology,* Houghton Mifflin Company, Boston, 1952.

Watson, R. I., *Psychology of the Child,* John Wiley and Sons, Inc., New York, 1959.

Wolff, W., *The Personality of the Pre-School Child,* Grune and Stratton, New York, 1947.

Chapter 13

Angrilli, A., "A Study of the Psychosexual Identification of Pre-School Boys," Ph.D. Dissertation, New York University, 1958.

Bartemeier, L., "The Contribution of the Father to the Mental Health of the Family," *American Journal of Psychiatry,* 1953, No. 110, pp. 277-280.

Cook, L. A. and Cook, E., *Sociological Approach to Education,* McGraw Hill, New York, 1950.

Dewey, J., *Experience and Education,* Macmillan Company, New York, 1953.

Despert, L. J., "The Fatherless Family," *Child Study Association of America,* Vol. 34, No. 3, Summer, 1957, pp. 22-28.

English, S. O. and Pearson, G. H., *Emotional Problems of Living,* George Allen and Unwin, London, 1947.

Gomberg, R., "Tomorrow's Family," *Child Study Association of America,* Vol. 34, No. 3, Summer, 1957, pp. 7-13.

Herbinière-Lebert, S., "L'éducation pré-scolaire, éducation de base," *L'Education Nationale,* No. 11, March, 1954, pp. 9-10.

Jersild, A. T. and Associates, *Child Development and the Cur-*

riculum, Bureau of Publications, Teachers' College, Columbia University, New York, 1946.

Joseph, H. and Zern, G., *The Emotional Problems of Children,* Crown Publishers Incorporated, New York, 1954.

Kanner, L., *Child Psychiatry,* C. C. Thomas, Springfield, Illinois, 1949.

Le Gall, A., *Caractérologie des enfants et des adolescents,* Presses Universitaires de France, Paris, 1950.

Piéron, H., "L'importance de la période pré-scolaire pour la formation d'esprit," *Cahiers de Pédagogie et d'Orientation Professionelle,* No. 2, September, 1954, pp. 52-59.

Pollak, O., *Integrating Sociological and Psychoanalytic Concepts,* Russell Sage Foundation, New York, 1956.

Russell, B., *On Education,* George Allen and Unwin, London, 1951.

Stone, L. J. and Church, J., *Childhood and Adolescence,* Random House, New York, 1957.

Wallon, H., "Milieu et enseignement decrolyen," *Archives Belges des Sciences de l'Education,* Vol. II, No. 3, January, 1937, pp. 173-175.

———, "Milieu familial et délinquence juvénile," *Pour l'Enfance "Coupable,"* January-February, 1940, pp. 3-5.

———, "Psychologie et éducation de l'enfance," *Pour l'Ere Nouvelle,* Vol. VI, No. 129, July, 1937, pp. 133-138.

Books for Children About Fathers and Other Men

Barr, J., *Mike the Milkman,* Albert Whitman and Company, Chicago, 1953.

Beim, J., *Country Train,* William Morrow and Company, New York, 1950.

Bianco, W. M., *The Hurdy-Gurdy Man,* Oxford University Press, New York, 1933.

Bontemps, A., *The Story of George Washington Carver,* Grosset and Dunlap, New York, 1954.

Brown, M., *Stone Soup,* Charles Scribner's Sons, New York, 1947.

Dalgliesh, A., *The Courage of Sarah Noble,* Charles Scribner's Sons, New York, 1954.

De Angeli, M., *The Coppertoed Boots,* Doubleday and Company, New York, 1938.

————, *Jared's Island,* Doubleday and Company, New York, 1947.

Deucher, S., Wheeler, O., *Sebastian Bach,* E. P. Dutton and Company, New York, 1937.

Earle, V., *The Busy Man,* Lothrop, Lee and Shepard, New York, 1951.

Ets, M. H., *Mr. T. W. Anthony Woo,* Viking Press, New York, 1951.

Gates, D., *Blue Window,* Viking Press, New York, 1940.

————, *My Brother Mike,* Viking Press, New York, 1948.

Gates, Huber, and Salisbury, *Mr. and Mrs. Big,* Macmillan Company, New York, 1951.

Leaf, M., *The Story of Ferdinand,* Viking Press, New York, 1945.

Lenski, L., *The Little Airplane,* Oxford University Press, New York, 1938.

———, *The Little Auto,* Oxford University Press, New York, 1934.

McCall, E., *Bucky Button,* Beckley-Cardy, Chicago, 1953.

———, *The Buttons at the Farm,* Beckley-Cardy, Chicago, 1955.

Norton, M., *The Borrowers,* Harcourt Brace, New York, 1953.

Pickard, V., *Mr. Hobs Can Fix It,* Abington-Cokesbury, New York, 1948.

Puner, Walker, *Daddies, What They Do All Day,* Lothrop, Lee and Shepard Company, New York, 1946.

Riesenberg, F., *Great Men of the Sea,* G. P. Putnam's Sons, New York, 1955.

Treeselt, A., *A Day With Daddy,* Lothrop, Lee and Shepard Company, New York, 1947.

Wilder, I. L., *Little House in the Big Woods,* Harper Brothers, New York, 1953.

———, *Little House in the Prairie,* Harper Brothers, New York, 1953.

———, *On the Banks of Plum Creek,* Harper Brothers, New York, 1953.

———, *Long Winter,* Harper Brothers, New York, 1953.

White, A. T., *The First Men in the World,* Random House, New York, 1953.

Index